The World of
SANDITON

The World of
SANDITON

SARA SHERIDAN

GRAND CENTRAL
PUBLISHING

NEW YORK BOSTON

CONTENTS

Welcome

My dear reader,

Welcome to the Regency seaside town of Sanditon in the year 1819.

This book gives you a peek behind the curtain of ITV's landmark production of Jane Austen's last, unfinished novel. Here you'll find interviews with the cast and crew and some of the fascinating real-life history of the people and places that inspired Austen's story.

Shot over the spring and summer of 2019 in the south of England, a team of hundreds brought Sanditon to life in the studio and on location in some of the many towns that were actually built along the shoreline during the Regency era.

We hope you enjoy the series, and this book: a celebration of Austen's unique, world-class talent that continues to inspire over 200 years after her death.

Yours, The Sanditon team

For Sanditon news, find updates online at:

Instagram — @Sanditon_official,

Facebook — @SanditonOfficial,

Twitter — @Sanditon

FOREWORD BY ANDREW DAVIES

In the last year of her life, Jane Austen embarked on a new novel, a bold departure from anything she had done before.

Of course, she provides us with a spirited young heroine and a fascinatingly complex and moody hero, but the setting is new, and the Parker brothers embody a new kind of Jane Austen character: they are men of affairs, entrepreneurs, men who want to change the world they live in and leave their mark on it. You could say it's a bit like Boardwalk Empire: Tom Parker is trying to develop a sleepy fishing village into a fashionable seaside resort. He's mortgaged his property to the hilt, borrowed from all and sundry, and now he's transforming Sanditon before our very eyes.

Young Charlotte Heywood comes to stay and falls in love with Sanditon and the whole enterprise. It's a different world for her, with a fascinating cast of characters: the eccentric and endearing Parker family; Lady Denham, the rich and domineering patroness; Sir Edward Denham and his step-sister Esther, whose relationship seems a little too close; Lady Denham's protégée Clara, the poor relation, who has something clandestine going on with Sir Edward – and

Miss Lambe, the heiress from the West Indies, Jane Austen's first black character! Mix in a few quarrels, schemes and misunderstandings, a couple of balls, and a bit of naked sea bathing (for the men) and we have a fascinating set of possibilities.

So far, so wonderful – but Austen's 60-page fragment only offered enough story material for half the first episode of what I hoped to develop as a returning eight-part series. Cue lots of research into the Regency era, and lots of imaginative brain-cudgelling. Lots of meetings with producers - executive producer Belinda Campbell and producer Georgina Lowe - and lots of jolly lunches. ITV wanted to go into production quickly, and there wasn't going to be enough time for me to write all eight scripts, so once the overall structure was set, we agreed that I would write the first three episodes and the last. From here on, everything happened bewilderingly quickly: Olly Blackburn, the director, and Grant Montgomery, the production designer, outlined their vision for the show, and soon we were casting, with established stars like Anne Reid, Kris Marshall and Theo James as well as exciting newcomers Rose Williams and Crystal Clarke as our heroine Charlotte and Miss Lambe.

At the time of writing this foreword we are halfway through filming, and I am thrilled with what we have achieved: a period drama that feels utterly fresh and modern – Jane Austen, but not as you knew her.

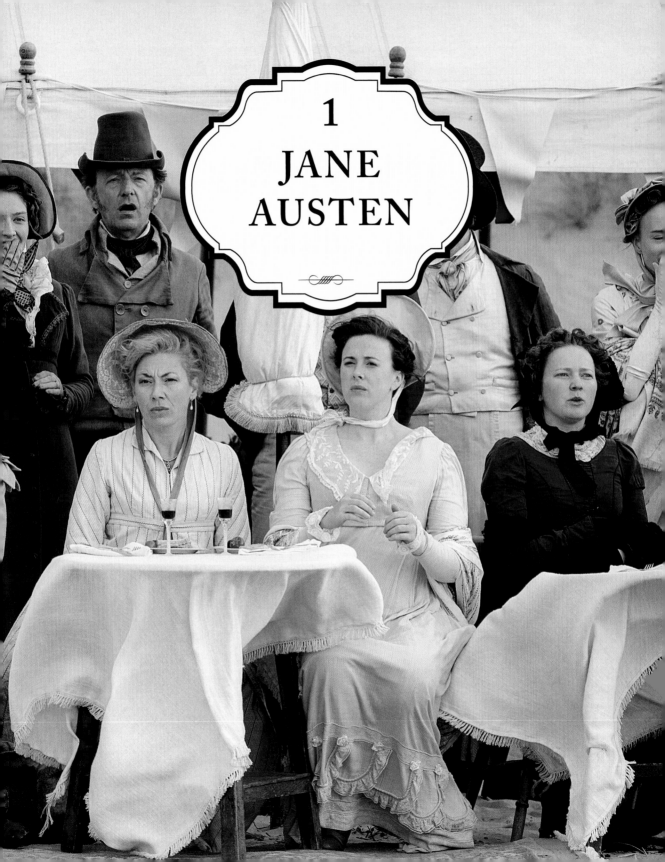

1
JANE
AUSTEN

· • • •

All about Jane

'I read the book as innocently as I can, at first. Just to see which bits I like.'

Andrew Davies,
screenwriter

THE MOST FAMOUS British female author in the world, Jane Austen's work is loved by millions, with devotees across the globe. Her books have remained in print for over two centuries with her most popular novel, *Pride and Prejudice*, selling 20 million copies alone. Austen was feted in her own era – the playwright Richard Sheridan said *Pride and Prejudice* was one of the cleverest things he'd ever read. Since their publication, almost all of Austen's stories have been adapted for film and TV, though this ITV production is the first ever of her last novel, *Sanditon*.

Austen's life belies her genius. Born on 16 December 1775, during the heyday of the Georgian era, Jane's love of words began at a young age when she started writing to entertain her close family. She and her older sister, Cassandra, were the only daughters of the Reverend George Austen and his wife, also Cassandra. The girls had six brothers. Growing up, Jane was an avid and witty letter writer, penning an estimated 3,000 letters over the course of her life – a huge correspondence, which was heavily edited and largely destroyed after her death by successive generations of the Austen family, who wanted to protect her memory. The material that is left paints a relatively subdued picture of her as a well-behaved spinster with only a few flashes of her caustic wit. Outspoken women were

Opposite: A portrait of Jane Austen.

not fashionable in Georgian or Victorian Britain, and it is thought that Jane's correspondence with her relations was considered too frank for public consumption. Today, fewer than 200 of her letters remain and most of those have been edited, so readers mainly know Jane's voice through her novels, which reveal her as a perceptive, funny and often forthright woman. A friend of Jane's brother, Henry, declared her novels 'much too clever to have been the work of a woman', thus underestimating one of the Regency era's most brilliant minds.

Engraving of Jane Austen and her sister Cassandra doing needlework in the rectory garden.

So where did this enduring favourite come from? We know quite a bit about Austen's family. Reverend George Austen, Jane's father, was known as 'the handsome proctor' during his time at St John's College, Oxford. After he married, he became the rector of the Anglican parishes of Deane and Steventon. Jane was born and grew up in the Steventon rectory in Hampshire. The parish was located in a sleepy valley surrounded by meadows and comprised around thirty families. Reverend Austen came from a successful wool manufacturing family but, as a younger son, he did not benefit from the family's wealth and had to earn his living. The job at Steventon was given to him by his much wealthier second cousin – a practice common at the time to help support less well-off relations. As well as being rector, the reverend earned extra money by farming and giving lessons to local children. This brought the family a total income of around £200 a year – over six times the average annual income for a working man, which was £30. However, it was also far less than the upwards of £1,000 that members of the aristocracy had at their disposal annually. Cassandra, Jane's mother, also came from a monied family, but her father was, like her husband, a rector, and although she had a small inheritance from her mother she was not a wealthy woman.

Despite the financial pressures, the Austens created a happy home where lively debate was encouraged. They got on with their wider family and, as well as writing to each other, they welcomed their relations on visits to Steventon. This brought news of foreign travel and fashionable London society into Jane's orbit from an early age. Even as a child, Jane wrote stories and often read these to her family in the evenings as an amusement. She was also a keen dancer – her older brother Henry said she 'excelled' at dancing. Dances and balls would have been held in neighbouring houses and at the local assembly rooms in the town hall in Steventon.

Women were not always educated in the Georgian era. A girl's chance of getting an education depended on the outlook of her parents, particularly her father. Luckily, Reverend Austen was open-minded and wanted his daughters to learn, as well as his sons. This was an additional financial commitment for him – schooling was not free. Despite this, at the age of eight Jane was sent to school with Cassandra (who was ten), first to Oxford and then to Southampton. Here, both girls caught typhus and were sent home to recover. Jane almost died and stayed at Steventon for over a year before her family found her a place at the Reading Abbey Girls' School, where she studied needlework, drama, French, dancing and music. However, the school fees proved too costly for the Austens' finances and both

Jane and Cassandra only attended for a couple of years. Thereafter, Jane was educated at home by her father and older brothers, something that could only be a successful arrangement in a close family, like the Austens. Young Jane was an avid reader who had free access to the family library (we know that during his university days, Reverend Austen owned over 500 books – probably more than that by the time Jane was old enough to read). Jane also had access to the library of eminent Austen family friend and neighbour, Warren Hastings, who was de facto Governor-General of India until 1785.

During her teenage years, Jane wrote three plays, as well as several poems and short stories. She drew heavily on what she was reading, lampooning popular novels and histories. She was always experimenting – and later collected 90,000 words of material from this period into three volumes now known as her 'Juvenilia'. It's easy to forget that many of Austen's heroines were close to Jane's age when she started to write. Lizzie Bennet in *Pride and Prejudice* is only twenty, Emma Woodhouse is twenty-one and Charlotte Heywood in *Sanditon* is in her late teens.

When Jane became an aunt for the first two times (in 1793 when her two eldest brothers both had daughters) she sent what she called 'scraps' to her new nieces – a short collection of writing to amuse them. Austen scholars have labelled Jane's early works as 'boisterous' and 'anarchic' and it is to Reverend Austen's credit that he did not try to tone down Jane's voice. In fact, he encouraged her, buying her a portable mahogany writing desk in 1794, which she used for the rest of her life. At the age of eighteen, Jane wrote her first adult novel, *Lady Susan*, which is told through a series of letters and is thought to be based on the story of Jane's sister-in-law,

'I'm sure Jane Austen would be delighted that her stories continue to have such resonance and such huge audiences today.'

Dr Hannah Greig,
historical consultant

Opposite: A page from the original manuscript of Persuasion *– 1816.*

With all this knowledge of Mr E.
& with this ~~authority to~~ impartiality it —
~~Anne quitted~~ Camdate Buildgs, — her
mind deeply busy in reviewing what she
had heard, feeling, thinking, recalling
& foreseeing everything, shocked ~~about~~
~~the Elliots~~, sighing over future. ~~She rejoiced~~
~~hained for Lady Russell~~, ~~& glorying in the~~
~~complacency~~ ~~of~~ ~~exposed complacency & had thrown off~~
~~that ~~ ~~of that ~~ ~~slength ~~
~~right & the ~~ ~~beauty, this add in~~
~~~~ ~~ ~~
~~~~ ~~Judged from~~ confidence
~~injun~~ had been entire. — ~~And~~ The Embarrass:
:ment which must be felt from their
~~horses~~ ~~~~ in his presence! — How to be
brave to him. — how to get rid of him —
what to do by any of the Party at
home. — where to be blind & where
to be active! — It was altogether a
confusion of Images & Doubts — a
perplexity, an ~~agitating~~ ~~embarasing~~ which
she could not see the end of.

And she was in Gay St. & still so ~~much~~
far engrossed, ~~as~~ that she started on
being addressed by Admiral Croft, as if a
person unlikely to be met there.

Eliza de Feuillide, whose first husband died on the guillotine during the French Revolution. Austen's career was underway.

'This little bag I hope will prove
To be not vainly made–
For, if you should a needle want
It will afford you aid.
And as we are about to part
T'will serve another end,
For when you look upon the Bag
You'll recollect your friend'

EARLY POEM BY JANE AUSTEN, THOUGHT TO HAVE
BEEN WRITTEN TO ACCOMPANY A GIFT

Jane never married but she had three romances. She fell in love with the first man at the age of twenty. It was a whirlwind. Thomas Lefroy visited Steventon for two months at the end of 1795 and into 1796 after completing his university degree. Lefroy was moving to London to take up a career as a barrister. The couple met at a social gathering and Jane wrote to Cassandra afterwards, 'I am most afraid to tell you how my Irish friend and I behaved. Imagine everything most shocking and profligate in the way of dancing and sitting down together.' In another letter Jane described Lefroy as 'good-looking' and 'very gentlemanlike'. Five days later she said she expected an offer from him (presumably of marriage) but declared she would refuse it. It seems the couple had genuinely fallen in love, but in Georgian England, for the middle and upper classes, money was more important than love when it came to marriage. Lefroy was dependent on a wealthy great-uncle and Jane had no money of her own

Thomas Lefroy.

and no dowry. We don't know if Thomas Lefroy proposed to Jane before he left Hampshire but, even if he had, she would (as she said) almost certainly have had to turn him down. As it was, his family intervened; Lefroy left and they never met again. Thomas Lefroy went on to have a hugely successful career and became Lord Chief Justice of Ireland.

> *'From now on, she [Jane] carried in her own flesh and blood, and not just gleaned from books and plays, the knowledge of sexual vulnerability: of what it is to be entranced by the dangerous stranger; to hope, and to feel the blood warm; to wince, to withdraw; to long for what you are not going to have and had better not mention. Her writing becomes informed by this knowledge, running like a dark undercurrent beneath the comedy.'*
>
> Claire Tomalin, Austen biographer

We don't know how Jane coped with the disappointment of parting from this young man, her first love, other than that she wrote to Cassandra that when she had to stop flirting with Lefroy (as she knew she must) there would be tears. After he left Steventon, the only letter in which she mentions him is dated almost three years later when she had tea with one of his relations and wanted to enquire about what he was up to but could not bring herself to form the words. Had she not still had feelings for him she might have been able to ask the question . . . For Lefroy's part, when he visited Hampshire, he never again went to Steventon or visited the Austen family. This was the savage reality of the English middle- and upper-class marriage market. In 1937 W. H. Auden would write of Austen, 'Beside her, Joyce seems innocent as grass.'

It was several years before Jane entered into another romance of any kind. In 1801 Reverend Austen retired and the family moved to Bath where Jane almost completely stopped writing. We don't know whether this was because she was unhappy or was simply much busier living in town than she had been in the country. The family enjoyed Bath and took regular trips to the nearby seaside during the summers they lived there, and this is where, in 1802, it seems Jane had a romantic entanglement with a minister called Dr Samuel Blackall. Blackall had shown an interest in Jane before, when he met her in Hampshire in 1798. When they bumped into each other, quite by chance, in Totnes in Devon (where Samuel's brother was the local doctor) he wrote to his friends saying he intended to pursue her. We don't know exactly how Jane felt about Samuel, though in her letters from the late 1790s she says she expects their relationship to 'decline in a reasonable manner', and she certainly doesn't refer to him with the passion and excitement she writes about Lefroy.

Far later, in July 1813, she mentions Blackall in a letter to her brother, Frank, as 'a piece of perfection – noisy perfection'. No letters remain from the summer of 1802, the actual time of the romance (raising the question as to why these letters were destroyed by the family), and it seems Jane was right – one way or another, the relationship came to nothing. Some Austen scholars believe that a poem Jane wrote about warring love rivals suggests that Cassandra, Jane's sister, was also keen on Dr Blackall. Whatever happened with the Austens, Blackall went on to marry a Miss

Lewis of Antigua and had no further contact with either Jane or Cassandra. However, the setting of a love rivalry in a seaside town, where visitors would have gone to recover their health, provides an intriguing real-life parallel to the world of *Sanditon*, as does the idea of a love interest with West Indian connections.

'It is the cause of many woes
It swells the eyes and reds the nose
And very often changes those
Who once were friends to bitter foes'

POEM ON LOVE BY JANE AUSTEN, WRITTEN IN 1807

With Lefroy and Blackall out of the picture, all was not lost in terms of Jane Austen's romantic prospects. In December 1802, Jane received an offer of marriage from the son of a family friend, Harris Bigg-Wither. The proposal came when she and Cassandra were visiting Harris's sisters at their home, Manydown, in Hampshire. Harris had recently come down from Oxford and was five years Jane's junior, but Jane had known him since they were children and, in Georgian terms, he was a good catch for her, the heir to a large family estate near Steventon. If she married Harris, Jane's money worries would be over and she could help her family by financially supporting her parents, Cassandra and her brothers.

Harris, though, was not appealing. He was not handsome and hardly ever spoke as he was prone to stuttering. When he did make conversation, he was awkward, came across as aggressive and lacked tact. His proposal presented a tricky dilemma – he was definitely not an ideal match personality-wise for fun-loving, communicative Jane. At first, however, she said yes, but the following morning she changed her mind and recanted on the engagement, leaving the Biggs's house that day by carriage, first to go to her brother's at nearby Steventon and then home to Bath. Jane's niece wrote afterwards: 'I have always respected her for the courage in cancelling that "yes". . . I beleive [sic] most young women so circumstanced would have taken Mr Wither and trusted to love after marriage.' Again, none of Jane's letters from this period survive, but later, when she gave romantic advice to her niece, Fanny Knight, she urged her not to commit herself unless she really liked the man and said: 'Anything is to be preferred or endured rather than marrying without affection.' It is advice she probably took herself the night she changed her mind about marrying Harris.

This, at the age of twenty-seven, was as far as we know the last time Jane entertained any kind of romantic involvement. In 1805 Jane's father died in Bath and four of her brothers stepped in to provide financially for her, Cassandra and their mother. Jane had already sold one book for a pittance by this time, but the publisher had decided simply to hold the rights for it and not actually publish. For the Austen women, there was never quite enough money and they struggled continually to cover their costs. The women moved several times over the next few years – from Bath to Steventon, from Steventon to Worthing and then on to Southampton, always in the company of their family friend, Martha Lloyd. Jane considered Martha a sister. The Lloyd family had lived nearby when Jane was growing up and occupied the empty manse at Reverend Austen's second parish at Deane, the use of which was within his gift. Martha had a sunny nature and enjoyed housekeeping as well as collecting recipes. After Jane's death, and in her sixties, she married Francis Austen (Jane and Cassandra's brother) and became Lady Austen. For now, though, she, like the Austen women, found herself in a difficult financial situation.

Deciding to stick together, Martha, Jane, Cassandra and old Mrs Austen spent their time visiting family and lived in straitened circumstances, only scraping by for several years. Jane continued to write during this time but nothing was published and it was unthinkable for a lady to get a job in order to earn her living, so the Austen women made do with what their menfolk could spare. This difficult period was alleviated in 1809 when Jane's brother Edward offered them the permanent use of a five-bedroom cottage in the village of Chawton in East Hampshire, in the beautiful South Downs, where he had inherited a large estate.

Chawton Cottage.

The cottage was originally a farmhouse, which briefly became a local pub in the 1780s, called the New Inn. It closed after two drink-fuelled murders on the premises and was subsequently let to the local bailiff. Then the Austen women moved in. Jane lived the last eight years of her life at Chawton, where she devoted herself to her writing, and it was here that four of her novels were finally published – *Pride and Prejudice*, *Sense and Sensibility*, *Mansfield Park* and *Emma*. The praise her work received, after such a long time, must have been exciting. Later, George Henry Lewes, the critic and long-term partner of George Eliot, said that he 'would rather have written *Pride and Prejudice*, or *Tom Jones*, than any of the Waverley Novels,' placing Jane higher in Lewes's estimation than Sir Walter Scott, the most famous novelist of the day.

However, the women lived quietly at Chawton, only entertaining family and teaching local poor children to read as well as running the house. The upside of this was that it left Jane a good deal of her time to spend writing on top of her household duties, which we know included being in charge of the sugar, tea and wine stores.

'Pride and Prejudice is my favourite. I played Mrs Bennet once in the theatre so I studied it. It's a beautiful book.'

Anne Reid, playing Lady Denham

'Our Chawton home how much we find
Already in it, to our mind;
And how convinced that when complete
It will all other Houses beat,
That ever have been made or mended,
With rooms concise or rooms distended.'

Jane Austen writing to her brother, Frank, in 1809, shortly after moving to Chawton

The atmosphere at Chawton when Jane lived there was later written about by Jane's nephew, James Edward Austen-Leigh, in his memoir: 'In that well-occupied female party, there must have been many precious hours of silence during which the pen was busy at the little mahogany writing desk, while Fanny Price, or Emma Woodhouse, or Anne Elliot was growing into beauty and interest.' While Jane received publishing payments during this period for her work, these were relatively small sums, though she was certainly much better off while living at Chawton than she had been at any time since her father's death. It must have felt liberating for her to earn her own money for the first time in her life.

Early in 1816 Jane began to feel unwell and gradually her health worsened. When her uncle died, leaving his fortune to his wife, thus disinheriting Jane's mother as well as Jane and Cassandra, she admitted that the shock and disappointment made her illness worse. The truth is that the Austen women during these last years of Jane's life never shook off the financial pressure of where the next pound might come from, and this financial stress took its toll on Jane's health. Her reported symptoms suggest that she was suffering from the adrenal illness Addison's disease, though some medical historians believe she may have had Hodgkin's disease, a form of cancer.

During Jane's last months, in early 1817, she wrote the first eleven chapters of *Sanditon*, stopping in March. It is unlikely that she realised she was going to die and she probably hoped that she would get over her illness. By April she was confined to bed and, in May, Cassandra and her brother Henry, helped by the Bigg sisters (Harris had by this time married someone else), took Jane to Winchester

'She was the sun of my life, the gilder of every pleasure, the soother of every sorrow. I had not a thought concealed from her, and it is as if I had lost a part of myself.'

Cassandra Austen following Jane's death

sixteen miles away, for medical treatment at the newly opened Winchester Hospital. She was in terrible pain and, in the end, she died in Cassandra's arms on 18 July 1817. She is buried in the north aisle of Winchester Cathedral where, today, there are three memorials to her. The first, her original gravestone, does not mention her writing – probably because it was not considered appropriate for a woman to have a profession. In 1870 her nephew raised a brass plaque to her memory, which starts: 'Jane Austen, known to many by her writings . . .', and in 1890 money was raised by private subscription to pay for a memorial window designed by Charles Eamer Kempe. She is now, without question, one of the most famous and well-loved novelists of all time with devotees worldwide.

'Austen broadened her canvas with Sanditon *– it was a departure from the usual style of her novels.'*

Dr Paula Byrne,
Jane Austen consultant

22	Braman	
	5 Stove	8 6
	1 lady	2 6
	Apels	9 11
	1 gate	1
	2 ledges	9
	30	

March
3
15 11

£ 3 5 8

1847
Nov. 27 204   c.

1848
Mar. 22 200   c.   26 00

Oct. 58 1848 Then let
Geo. H. Braman and

1849
Nov. 9 213   c.   85
April 25 214   "   30 00   By thirty Dollar
June 4 215   "   4 30   Ah. accounts for in last
July 28 216   "   3 33   Settlement
Oct. 2 217   "   17 75
" 12 218   "   22 84
" 24 219   2 41
                          31 48   Settled

Trafalgar House Accounts

No. 361

Treasury-Office, Aug. 17th 1789.

I CERTIFY That Capt. Asa Upson
has lodged in this Office the following Notes, viz.
Army Notes due June 1, 1785, amounting to | 11 | 2 | 0¾
Ditto — — 1786,
Ditto — — 1787,
Ditto — — 1788,
Ditto — — 1789,

Ditto per Ditto, payable to the Bearer,
Ditto per Act of May 1783, &c.
Amounting to £. | 29 | 13 | 2¾
For which I have issued 1 Notes for | 28 | 1
Leaving the Sum of .... | 1
| 2

For which he is entitled to receive Certificat...
suance of an Act of the General Assembly...
1789.

.3 75.

Sd.

6 01
1 50
12 00
21 96
8 50   # 49 99
49 97 Settled Nov. 12 47847

12 65² Dec.   Settled   12 65

JANE AUSTEN TIMELINE

· • • • ·

16 DECEMBER 1775: Jane born at Steventon Rectory, Hampshire, England, to Reverend George Austen and Cassandra Austen (née Leigh).

1783: Jane catches typhus in Southampton after being sent away to school. She barely survives.

1783–85: Jane is home-schooled.

1785–86: Jane attends Reading Abbey Girls' School.

1787–93: Jane writes poems, stories and plays for her family.

1793–95: Jane writes her first full-length work, the epistolary novel *Lady Susan*.

1795–96: Jane's romance with Thomas Lefroy.

1797: Jane sells the copyright to *Northanger Abbey*, but the book is not published.

1801: The Austen family move to Bath.

1802: Jane is pursued by Dr Samuel Blackall.

1802: Jane receives a proposal of marriage from Harris Bigg-Wither.

1804: Jane starts to write her unfinished novel, *The Watsons*.

1805: Reverend George Austen, Jane's father, dies.

1805: The Austen women move to Worthing.

1806: The Austen women move to Southampton.

1809: The Austen women move to Chawton.

1811: Publication of *Sense and Sensibility*, Jane's first novel to be published. The title page says it was written 'By a Lady'.

1813: *Pride and Prejudice* published.

1814: *Mansfield Park* published.

1815: Jane invited to visit the Prince Regent's London residence and dedicate *Emma* to him.

1815: *Emma* published.

JANUARY 1817: Jane starts to write *The Brothers* (later named *Sanditon*).

MARCH 1817: Jane stops writing as her illness progresses.

18 JULY 1817: Jane dies in Winchester, Hampshire, England.

1818: *Persuasion* and *Northanger Abbey* published as a set and Jane is named for the first time as the author.

· • • • ·

Getting published in the Georgian era

'For the truth is that every true admirer of the novels cherishes the happy thought that he alone – reading between the lines – has become the secret friend of their author.'

Katherine Mansfield

Until well into the eighteenth century, there was no such thing as a publisher. Booksellers and writers arranged for work to be printed and distributed without the intervention of a professional to select, edit and design books. Some of the greatest writers in the world published their own material, which was often then copied without payment. William Shakespeare's plays, for example, appeared in his own lifetime in a variety of 'pirate' editions. Robert Burns published his poetry 'by subscription', which worked like a modern crowdfunder: readers paid up front for their copy of the book and Burns only went to print once he had raised enough money to do so.

Austen, however, was one of the first generation of writers to be able to submit their manuscripts to a publisher, as the fledgling industry established itself. In middle-class Georgian society it was considered pushy or showy for ladies to put their work forward and the idea of women writing as a 'job' was unattractive. In addition, married women were not 'legal entities' and could not sign contracts – effectively, they belonged to their husbands. While widows and single women were able to contract, it was frowned on and commonly women were the legal responsibility of their male relations (fathers or brothers). Austen never published under her own name during her lifetime and submissions to her publishers were managed by her male relations. In this she was lucky – the men in some families would not have been open-minded enough to allow their womenfolk to publish their work. Over time, Jane established a relationship directly with her publishers and wrote to them about matters such as dedications and print times (though never contracts).

As today, different kinds of publishing deals were available. A publisher could buy the copyright to a work so that they would then own it outright. Or the work could be produced 'on commission', which meant that the publisher advanced the money to print and distribute the book and then repaid themselves from its sales. Once the costs were covered, the publisher retained ten per cent of the book's income with ninety per cent going back to the author. If, however, the book did not sell enough copies to cover its costs, the author was liable for the shortfall. All publishers in this era were individual, small companies run by one or two businessmen and often handed down from father to son.

'The person, be it gentleman or lady, who has not pleasure in a good novel must be intolerably stupid.'

Mr Tilney,
Northanger Abbey

declined by Return of Post.

Sir

I have in my possession a Manuscript Novel, comprised in three Vol.s about the length of Miss Burney's Evelina. As I am well aware of what consequence it is that a work of this sort should make its first Appearance under a respec: :table name I apply to you. Shall be much obliged therefore if you will inform me whether you chuse to be concerned in it; what will be the expence of publishing at the Authors risk, & what you will venture to advance for the Property of it, if on a perusal it is approved of.

Should your answer give me encouragement I will send you the Work.

I am, Sir, y.r ob.t hble Serv.t

Geo Austen.

Steventon near Overton
Hants
1.st Nov.r 1797.

Like all writers, Austen had rejections. The established publisher Thomas Cadell turned down *Pride and Prejudice* in 1797 by return of post – potentially the worst publishing decision in history. Jane's father had submitted the manuscript on her behalf and we do not know if Jane was even aware that he had done so. Jane's first success came in 1803 when publisher Benjamin Crosby bought the copyright to an early draft of *Northanger Abbey* for £10. Crosby never published the book despite Jane pushing him to bring it out. He never gave a reason why he decided to withhold the manuscript from the market, and in the end Jane ended up buying back the copyright thirteen years later with the intention of organising its publication elsewhere. Jane's first novel to be published was released in late 1811 when Thomas Egerton published *Sense and Sensibility* from his offices in Charing Cross in London. Jane's brother Henry underwrote the printing costs. Copies of this first edition had sold out by 1813. Egerton went on to publish *Pride and Prejudice* (which sold for the sum of eighteen shillings a copy – three shillings more than *Sense and Sensibility*, with Egerton capitalizing on the popularity of Jane's first novel) and then *Mansfield Park*. At this stage in her career, cheap pirate copies of Jane's books appeared in translation in French.

In 1815 Jane moved publisher to John Murray, whose grand house in Albemarle Street in Piccadilly was the centre of the literary world. Murray hosted a lavish salon and published London's most famous and glamorous writers, including Lord Byron. He brought out both *Emma* and a second edition of *Mansfield Park* to great acclaim and,

A letter to the publisher Thomas Cadell from Jane Austen's father offering Pride and Prejudice which was turned down via post.

after Jane's death, *Persuasion* and *Northanger Abbey*. Though they never met in person, Jane became friends with Murray, borrowing reading materials from his extensive library, and sending letters to complain about the printer being slow in producing her books.

Jane's novels were popular (with large print runs for the period – up to around 2,000 copies at a time) but she did not make a huge amount of money from her work. The first edition of *Sense and Sensibility* earned her £140. She then sold the copyright to *Pride and Prejudice* outright for £110. This sum was not inconsiderable at the time but it was not enough for a lady to live on indefinitely. Her biggest earner was *Mansfield Park*, which was published in 1814 and sold out its first edition in six months. Sadly, later editions of the book did not do as well and ended up swallowing most of Jane's profits from *Emma*.

A first edition of
Pride and Prejudice.

PRIDE

AND

PREJUDICE:

A NOVEL.

IN THREE VOLUMES.

BY THE
AUTHOR OF " SENSE AND SENSIBILITY."

VOL. I.

London:
PRINTED FOR T. EGERTON,
MILITARY LIBRARY, WHITEHALL.
1813.

· • • • ·

The royal stamp
of approval

As today, Britain was a constitutional monarchy during the Regency and the royal family had a huge influence on public opinion. This did not always mean that they were popular but royal taste certainly had an impact on society. An important element of this influence were the likes and interests of royal women. Charlotte of Mecklenburg-Strelitz was George III's wife and queen from 1761 to 1818 (all of Austen's life); she was the first member of the royal family to live in what we now call Buckingham Palace (known then as Buckingham House). Charlotte felt a certain kinship with other women and, in 1789, at the outbreak of the French Revolution, the queen ordered apartments to be readied for the queen of France, Marie Antoinette, with whom she corresponded.

Queen Charlotte was well educated and a keen amateur botanist whose marriage was marred by her husband's bouts of 'madness'. The mother of fifteen, the queen struggled in her relationship with her eldest son, George, Prince of Wales, who formally became regent in 1811 when the king's illness rendered him unfit to rule. Many people had sympathy with the queen and, although Jane Austen was invited to dedicate her novel *Emma* to the Prince Regent in 1815, we

'To his Royal Highness, the Prince Regent, this work is, by His Royal Highness's Permission, most Respectfully Dedicated by his Royal Highness's Dutiful and Obedient Humble Servant.'

Jane Austen, dedication of *Emma* to the Prince Regent

know that she did not approve of his lifestyle. The prince, by contrast, was definitely a long-standing Austen fan, buying a copy of *Sense and Sensibility* from London booksellers Becket and Porter for the full cover price of fifteen shillings on 28 October 1811, two days before the novel was officially advertised for sale. He kept copies of Austen's books in all his royal residences.

Austen's dedication to the prince was polite but unenthusiastic, and she resisted suggestions by the regent's librarian, Reverend James Stanier Clarke, who encouraged her to write a romance set in the House of Coburg (the regent's royal house). In 1813 Austen wrote in her letters about her sympathy for Caroline of Brunswick, the prince's wife, when the truth about the sham of their royal marriage came out. 'Poor woman, I shall support her as long as I can, because she *is* a Woman, & because I hate her Husband,' she said.

Austen's stance was pragmatic and there is no doubt that the royal dedication helped popularise *Emma*. Hanoverian royals were hugely influential culturally. George III and Charlotte founded key strands in what is now the Royal Collection (the largest art collection in the world), and despite Jane's antipathy, the regent's support was a coup for her as a writer. Queen Charlotte was also known to support women in the arts and, unusually, made a point of commissioning portraits by female artists, including Mary Delany and Mary Knowles. She also encouraged her daughters' artistic talents despite the prejudices against women putting their creative work up for sale and exhibiting publicly. These kinds of royal statements were important in legitimising female artists and creatives by normalising their work.

· • • • ·

Women of words:
Jane's inspiration and
her rivals

Being a female writer in the Georgian era was not easy but Jane was not alone. Several women enjoyed highly successful careers in fiction and non-fiction, and there is no doubt that Jane read and was influenced by their books.

· • • • ·

MARY WOLLSTONECRAFT
(1759–1797)

Non-fiction: A Vindication of
the Rights of Woman *(1792)*

―――――――

A searing intellect who wrote one of the earliest works of feminist philosophy, Mary Wollstonecraft was famous when Austen was a child. Judged harshly for generations because of life choices considered immoral at the time, coupled with her suicide, Wollstonecraft's work was commonly lampooned. However, though Austen never mentioned Wollstonecraft by name, some of the main themes of her work appear in Austen's novels. The character of the dashing Mr Wickham in *Pride and Prejudice* echoes the exact description given by Wollstonecraft of the kind of men standing armies produce (unprincipled and manipulative) and Elizabeth Bennet's criticism of 'female accomplishments' mirror Wollstonecraft's comments on the same subject. The similarities that

Austen observes between slavery and the treatment of women in Georgian society is one of Wollstonecraft's favourite themes. Jane's character Anne Elliot in *Persuasion* proves more adept at managing the family estate than her father and it is classic Wollstonecraft to point out women being more competent than their menfolk. Had Austen lived into her forties she would have read the seminal novel by Wollstonecraft's daughter, Mary Shelley – *Frankenstein*.

MARY BRUNTON (1778–1818)

Novels: Self-Control *(1811) and* Discipline *(1814)*

A Methodist, Mary Brunton eloped from her family home in Orkney to marry a Church of Scotland minister to whom her mother objected. The couple moved to Edinburgh where Brunton's husband took up a post as Professor of Oriental Languages at the university and Mary began to write. Her work was hugely successful during her lifetime, though, sadly, she died in childbirth without completing her third novel, *Emmeline*. In her letters, Austen describes Brunton's debut as an 'excellently-meant, elegantly-written work, without anything of Nature or Probability in it'. However, Austen's character Emma Woodhouse, heroine of the

eponymous *Emma*, owes a lot to Brunton's spoilt but ultimately loveable Ellen Percy in her second novel, *Discipline*. Austen never credited Brunton's influence, saying she had created in Emma 'a heroine whom no-one but myself will much like', but the parallels are striking and the timing of publication perfect for this sister novelist to have inspired one of Austen's most well-loved heroines.

FRANCES BURNEY
(1752–1840)

Novels: Evelina *(1778)*, Cecilia *(1782)*,
Camilla *(1796)*, The Wanderer *(1814)*

————————

A brilliant satirist who wrote plays and non-fiction as well as novels, Burney's character Dr Lyster and his comment in the final pages of her novel *Cecilia* is said to have inspired Austen to use the title *Pride and Prejudice*. Burney also used the device of letters as a way of telling her stories, a technique mirrored by Austen in her first novel, *Lady Susan*, and in some chapters of *Pride and Prejudice*. While Austen never left England, Burney lived an exciting life, spending time in France and also surviving a mastectomy, which was administered without the aid of anaesthetic.

MARIA EDGEWORTH (1768–1849)

Novels: Castle Rackrent *(1800)*, Belinda *(1801)*, Leonora *(1806)*, Ennui *(1809)*, The Absentee *(1812)*, Patronage *(1814)*, Harrington *(1817)*, Ormond *(1817)*

A member of the Anglo-Irish gentry, Maria Edgeworth was the most commercially successful novelist of the Georgian age, who also wrote non-fiction. All of her writing focused on moral education. Jane admired Edgeworth's work so much that she gifted her a copy of *Emma* when it was published in 1815, but Edgeworth never acknowledged this and seemingly didn't enjoy the book, later writing there was 'no story in it'. Austen mentions some of Edgeworth's novels in *Northanger Abbey*, saying they were works in which 'the greatest power of the mind is displayed'. In *Sanditon*, the character of Georgiana Lambe may well have been inspired by Edgeworth's *Belinda*, in which she wrote of a marriage between an African slave and an English farm girl, which was edited out of later editions.

Jane Austen's FAMILY TREE

William Austen (1701–1737)
m. Rebecca Walter (*née* Hampson)

Tysoe Saul Hancock
(*d.* 1775)
m. Philadelphia
(1730–1792)

Rev. George
(1731–1805)
m. Cassandra Leigh
(1739–1827)

Leonora
(1732–1783)

Eliza (Elizabeth) (1761–1813)
m.1 Jean Capot de Feuillide (*guillotined* 1794)
m. 2 Henry Austen (*brother of Jane Austen*)

George
(1766–1838)

Cassandra
(1773–1845)

Francis (1774–1865)
m. Mary Gibson

Rev. James
(1765–1819)
m.1
Anne Matthew
(*d.* 1795)

Edward
(1767–1852)
m. Elizabeth
Bridges

Henry
(1797–1843)

11 children

1 child

11 children

JANE
(1775–1817)

Charles (1779–1852)
m.1 Frances Palmer
m. 2 Harriet Palmer

m. 2
Mary Lloyd
(1771–1843)

4 children

4 children

2 children

· • • ·

Jane's legacy

Apart from a short time after her death, when it seems the family were simply grieving and were not minded to organise Jane's affairs with publishers, Jane Austen's work has never been out of print. Her writing grew in the public consciousness from the time of her death and was increasingly popular during the Victorian age, into the twentieth century and beyond, with television and film adaptations introducing swathes of new Austen fans to her stories. Everyone on the team at *Sanditon*, from writers to producers to directors and actors, has been inspired by her story. As the popularity of her books has grown, so has a fascination with her life, and for over a century there has been a lively market in Jane memorabilia and artefacts, housed in both public and private collections.

LETTERS

Quite apart from the destruction and editing of her correspondence by her family in the decades following her death, some of Jane's letters were cut up and sold as mementos of the great writer's hand. The market in Jane letters is still strong, with a letter to her favourite niece, Anna Lefroy, dated 29 October 1812, selling at Sotheby's in London in

Opposite A letter from Jane Austen to her brother Frank after the death of their father..

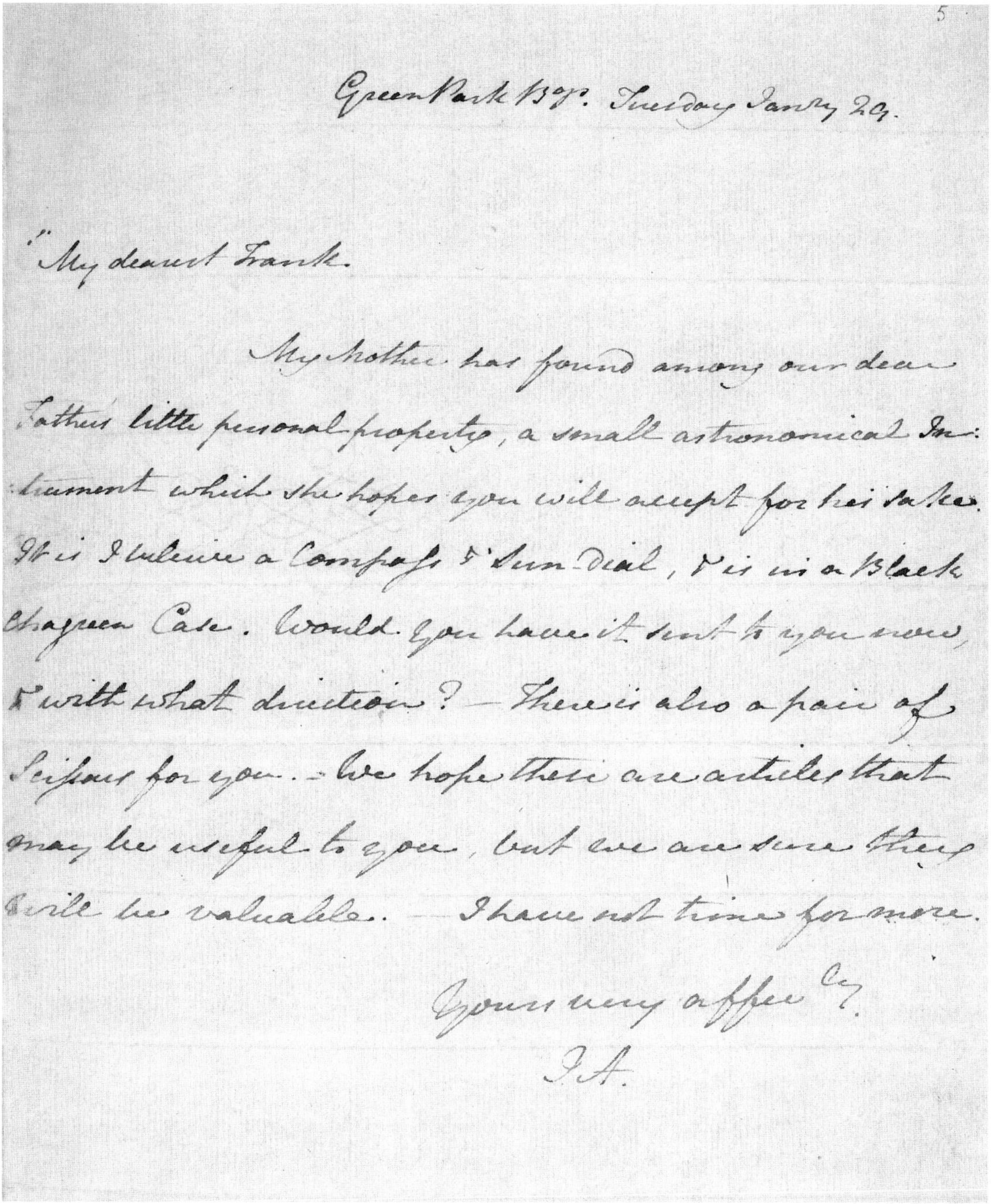

5

Green Park Bldgs. Tuesday Jan.y 2.d.

"My dearest Frank.

My Mother has found among our dear Father's little personal property, a small astronomical In=strument which she hopes you will accept for her sake. It is I believe a Compass & Sun-Dial, & is in a Black Chagreen Case. Would you have it sent to you now, & with what direction? — There is also a pair of Scissors for you. — We hope these are articles that may be useful to you, but we are sure they will be valuable. — I have not time for more.

Yours very affec.ly

J.A.

July 2017 for £162,500. This letter is particularly interesting because in it Jane criticises a novel by her contemporary, Rachel Hunter, as 'tiresome and prosy'. It sheds light on what she was reading and what she valued in a novel.

'I should have begun my letter soon after our arrival but for a little adventure which prevented me. After we had been here a quarter of an hour it was discovered that my writing and dressing boxes had been by accident put into a chaise which was just packing off as we came in, and were driven away towards Gravesend in their way to the West Indies. No part of my property miles off.'

Jane Austen to Cassandra Austen, 24 October 1798.

WRITING DESK

Jane's writing desk was given to her by her father in December 1794. He chose a portable mahogany writing box, which opens into a sloping surface, inlaid with leather. The box has a drawer with space for quills, ink and a penknife for cutting nibs. Reverend Austen bought the desk from Ring Brothers in Basingstoke, probably as Jane's twentieth birthday present, and we know she wrote many of her books sitting at this little desk. After her death, the box passed to Cassandra and then down the female line of the Austen family until 1999, when it was gifted to the British Library in London, where it is on display.

Jane Austen's writing desk.

JANE AUSTEN'S HOUSE MUSEUM

The cottage at Chawton where Jane lived for the last years of her life became the Jane Austen's House Museum in 1947 and is visited by around 40,000 people a year. The museum houses a collection of objects from Jane's life. These include Reverend Austen's glass-fronted bookcase, the table on which Jane's portable writing desk sat, a beautiful patchwork quilt that the Austen women worked on during 1811, silhouettes of Reverend and Cassandra Austen, as well as many books, letters and sheet music that belonged to the family. After Jane's death, her sister Cassandra cut some locks of her hair and the museum also has a gold mourning locket containing this hair. Hair jewellery was common during the Regency period and was used as a way of remembering a loved one. Cassandra inherited Jane's jewellery and the museum has a gold ring with a turquoise stone and two topaz crosses set in gold, which were given to Jane and Cassandra by their younger brother Charles in 1801. It is also possible to visit nearby, what Jane called 'the Great house' or Chawton House, where Jane's brother, Edward lived. As well as a library of books by female writers and a collection of early Austen manuscripts, Chawton House is now home to the Jane Austen Garden Trail. Jane loved walking in the gardens and often mentions doing so in her letters.

A gold and turquoise ring which belonged to Jane Austen.

'He has been buying Gold chains and Topaze [sic] Crosses for us; – he must be well scolded . . . I shall write again by this post to thank and reproach him. We shall be unbearably fine.'

Jane Austen to Cassandra Austen, 27 May 1801

'I went up to the Great House between 3 and 4, and dawdled an hour away very comfortably'

Jane Austen 1814
Jane Austen to Cassandra Austen, 24 October 1798

THE RICE PORTRAIT

'Have you remembered to collect peices [sic] for the patchwork?'

Jane Austen to Cassandra Austen, 31 May 1811

The portrait in oils by Ozias Humphry was painted in 1788 and shows a young girl wearing a Regency-style muslin dress and holding a green parasol. Owned by the Rice family, who are descendants of Austen, it is believed that it might be an early image of Jane, although this is hotly contested and has never been proved. If true, it is a fascinating image of the author in a pretty, fashionable muslin frock. Jane would have been thirteen at the time of the painting's execution.

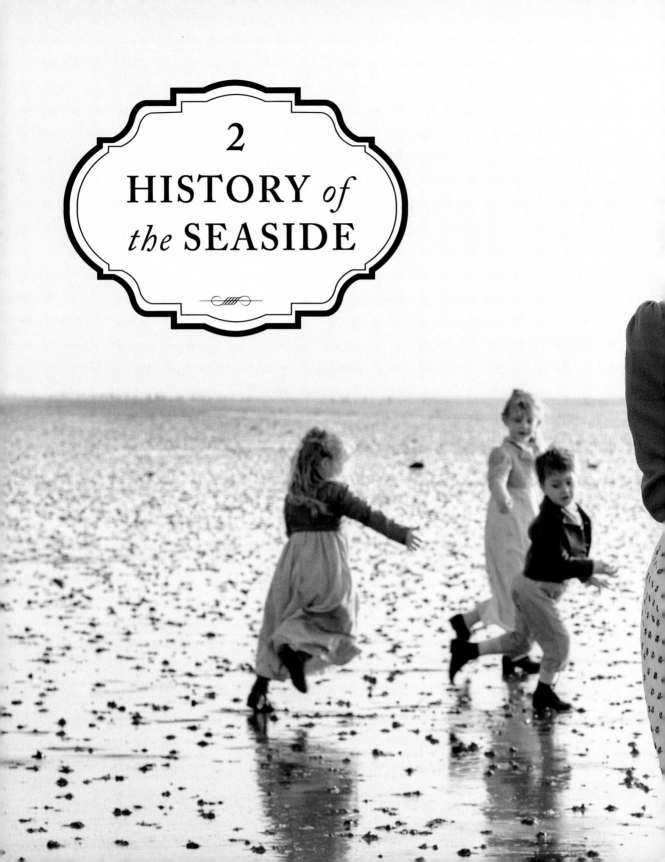

2
HISTORY *of*
the SEASIDE

·　●　●　●　·

SANDITON WAS BORN of a Regency phenomenon
– the seaside holiday. Britain is an island nation
with several thousand miles of coastline, so when,
during the Napoleonic Wars, people were encouraged to
holiday at home rather than travel to continental Europe
(with all its military action), the seaside was the obvious
place for the middle and upper classes to spend their sum-

Margate beach circa 1890.

mers. Before the days of rail travel, moving from one place to another was out of the financial reach of the majority of the population. Later, as the Victorian working classes bought bicycles and benefited from affordable awaydays by rail, the upper classes chose to holiday in more inaccessible locations. Queen Victoria built her holiday home on the Isle of Wight, having bought the Osborne estate in 1845 – a resort that could only be reached by boat (or, in her case,

The Royal Pavilion in Brighton.

royal yacht) – and in 1852 Prince Albert purchased the Balmoral estate in the inaccessible Highlands of Scotland for the royal family to use in privacy. The queen disliked visiting Brighton because there were too many ordinary people in close proximity and sold George IV's Brighton Pavilion in 1850, declaring it too small for her growing family and its gardens and central location too accessible to prying eyes. In the Regency, however, such issues with privacy weren't the case, and the expense of travelling kept resorts exclusive, allowing the upper-class vogue for holidays in spa towns and seaside resorts to flourish.

LADY DENHAM: And our bathing machines at Sanditon are the best on the whole of the south coast! *Episode 1*

The seaside was not only popular with the British upper classes on holiday, though. Fleeing French aristocrats often settled along the south coast of England, some subsidised generously by the British government. When the Duc de Bourbon escaped the guillotine in Paris in 1789 during the French Revolution, he took a house on the south coast (reputedly within sight of his beloved homeland) and, in 1830, in the uprisings of the following generation, King Charles X of France fled initially to Poole, in Dorset, though ultimately William IV provided him with accommodation far further north, at the Palace of Holyroodhouse in Edinburgh. These French émigrés added a sophisticated dimension to seaside society, as the aristocrats brought with them their own staff, such as dressmakers and chefs, and made use of the skills of small groups of French Huguenots who had settled along the south coast over a century before. These immigrants were mostly talented craftspeople and their skills as enamellers and weavers of silk had been passed down through the generations.

'The admired spot, the favourite summer residence of numerous families of distinction . . . Possessing every convenience . . . having good bathing machines and a fine sandy beach. His late majesty, George IV, honoured this spot with a visit . . . The air here is salubrious . . . these qualities were appreciated and emphatically remarked on by His Majesty George II.'

Guidebook to Mudeford, 1835

Such a cultural mix made seaside society smart. In addition, London was an international city with a thriving port and a growing population. In 1815 over 1.2 million

The ESPLANADE

A caricature entitled 'George III on the Esplanade at Weymouth'.

people lived in the capital, compared to New York in 1810, where the population reached only 96,000 The result of this influx was that seaside and holiday towns were subject to visits from foreign tourists, and that many upper- and middle-class homes employed skilled labour from abroad.

Imports such as tea, coffee and chocolate were common in wealthy homes and the novelty of imported goods provided an exotic social focus – like the pineapple lunch thrown in Sanditon. All this created a glamorous mixture that enticed people towards the shore.

An unexpected result of the cosmopolitan milieu of the season in some English resorts was that the concept was exported to other places, particularly within Europe. As visitors took home with them the ideas they'd enjoyed most, they created versions of English holiday resorts wherever they lived, and these sprang up across Europe through the whole of the nineteenth century, with continental towns adapting to fit in with local bathing practices and sensibilities. British visitors abroad in the mid-1800s commented on the availability of goods and services on a Sunday in these continental resorts. In many British seaside settlements, everything simply shut down on the Sabbath. While the spa town originated in Germany, the seaside resort was a very British idea that spread worldwide quickly.

'Nobody could catch cold by the sea; nobody wanted appetite by the sea; nobody wanted spirits; nobody wanted strength. Sea air was healing, softening, relaxing – fortifying and bracing – seemingly just as was wanted – sometimes one, sometimes the other. If the sea breeze failed, the seabath was the certain corrective; and where bathing disagreed, the sea air alone was evidently designed by nature for the cure.'

Sanditon

· • • • ·

On doctor's orders

TOM PARKER: Now we are coming near! Do you feel a difference in the air, Miss Heywood? Sea air! Better than any medicine or tonic! *Episode 1*

LADY DENHAM: What are you talking about over there?

CLARA: Sea-bathing, Lady Denham.

LADY DENHAM: Excellent! Nothing better for a young woman's circulation! *Episode 1*

"'If one could but go to Brighton!" observed Mrs Bennet.

"Oh, yes! If one could but go to Brighton! But Papa is so disagreeable."

"A little sea-bathing would set me up for ever."'

Pride and Prejudice

As well as the views (for ladies, the pastime of painting the seaside vista was a popular pursuit) and the cosmopolitan nature of seaside society in successful resorts, holidaymakers chose the seaside for another reason: their health. In the era before anaesthesia and penicillin, doctors' capabilities were limited. Surgery was at best basic and at worst butchery.

In 1752 Dr Richard Russell published his *Dissertation on the Use of Sea-Water in the Diseases of the Glands*. This book proposed both sea bathing and the drinking of seawater for medicinal purposes, not only to cure illness but as a prophy-

'Every five years, one hears of some new place or other starting up by the sea and growing the fashion. How they can half of them be filled is the wonder!'

Sanditon

lactic to guard against it. After the publication of this theory, the seaside was popularly seen as beneficial to health, with sea bathing encouraged and 'taking the air' or 'ozone' prescribed for a wide variety of illnesses. Drinking sea or spa water was referred to as 'taking the cure'. The reality was that, sadly, in the Regency era, there was no cure for most disease and people died from complaints that today would not be considered serious. Compared to much of what was medically available, the seaside offered the restorative hope of a cure without either great pain or much chance of actually worsening the patient's condition, and invalids flocked to the coast as a result. The regent's father, George III, when he first became 'mad', visited Weymouth where he bathed in the sea while a band played 'God Save the King' on the beach nearby. Resorts encouraged health tourists in any way they could – Boscombe developed its own clifftop mineral spa, while Bournemouth hotels imported French mineral water, which they encouraged visitors to drink for its supposed health benefits. In fairness, London, particularly in high summer, was crowded and dirty. The River Thames was a major arterial route and was extremely polluted, so going to the seaside may have had some health benefits for Georgian invalids. Although sea bathing and the drinking of seawater were not efficacious, modern medical studies have shown that mental health benefits can be derived from the sea air, which contains heightened levels of minerals.

· • • ·

Architecture on the coast:
seaside style

Investors, like Tom Parker in *Sanditon*, were quick to snap up opportunities in small towns along the south coast as escape to the seaside became more and more fashionable. They built houses to let to wealthy holidaymakers and, in order to make them attractive, emulated all the latest architectural trends in London. Regency architecture is distinctive, with the first professional architects (as opposed to

The Royal Pavilion, 1818.

builders) coming to the fore in the late eighteenth century and developing the neo-classical style. This was based on the study of classical Greek and Roman design, but in the Regency take on the style buildings were decorated with what were at the time modern motifs. The next generation of architects included the Prince Regent's own architect, John Nash, who popularised 'stucco' – a pale cement rendering, which, applied over brick, looked like stone. Nash designed Buckingham Palace, still the residence of the British monarch, as well as the regent's own place by the sea, the exotic Brighton Pavilion.

For less noble but still upper-class visitors, investors built terraces of smart houses rather than detached or semi-detached residences. This maximised sea views, which were at a premium. They also chose long windows, sometimes with ornate wrought-iron balconies, and constructed space-efficient bows to accommodate more glass and hence capture the optimum amount of light and the best vistas. Seaside development was largely a good investment, and buff, white or cream stucco terraces dominate the central areas of seaside towns on the south coast of England to this day, the boom really taking off at the end of the Napoleonic War in 1815 – just before *Sanditon* is set. Like Tom Parker, investors worked speculatively, hoping to rent or sell their buildings once they were completed, though sometimes this worked against them. In 1793 several banks in Bath went bankrupt and this led to plans for development being mothballed. There was no public protection and builders who were engaged in projects funded by these banks lost everything, so for several years development in the city ceased.

'*The beach at low water extends six miles and at ebb-tide is generally five hours, by which the ladies and gentleman take delightful rides and walks, and in other parts it is occupied by some of the best cricket players in England, the sands being so fine and level ... From the fineness of the morning, as early as six o'clock, the sands were crowded with fashionable families. After breakfast the beach and the sands were crowded with barouches [four wheeled horse-drawn carriages, curricles (open two-wheeled carriage], ponies and donkeys.*'

Contemporary description of Worthing in 1805

Where they worked, however, new developments fired population growth in seaside towns and this increased more quickly than in other British towns of the era as businesses moved in to service the holidaymakers and other residents. When we first visit Sanditon in the TV production this is certainly the case – Tom Parker is obsessed with bringing more and more people to the town to ensure its success. This is absolutely in line with what was happening in real life at this time. As an example, Margate's population rose by sixty-five per cent between 1801 and 1820 – almost double the overall average population increase across England in the same period, which ran at the impressive rate of thirty-five per cent. This was great for local residents, who had often originally made their living by fishing or running the kind of small businesses that village settlements could sustain – a local pub, for example. As a town grew, entrepreneurial locals often invested their own money, growing their businesses to take advantage of wealthy visitors. In Brighton,

"'Civilization, civilization indeed!" cried Mr Parker, delighted. "Look, my dear Mary, look at William Heeley's windows. Blue shoes, and nankin boots! Who would have expected such a sight at a shoemaker's in old Sanditon! This is new within the month. There was no blue shoe when we passed this way a month ago. Glorious indeed!"'

Sanditon

for example, several innkeepers opened bathhouses offering both hot and cold baths, which were believed to be good for different medical conditions. Small grocery shops expanded into far larger stores and began stocking luxury goods and souvenirs to attract upper-class custom – like the blue shoes in Heeley's. In little more than a decade a place might be transformed – going from a sleepy seaside fishing village to a sophisticated town with many amenities.

Mahomed's Indian vapour baths on the seafront at Brighton

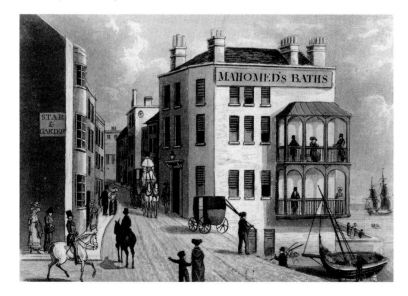

At a public level, local councils worked with investors to increase facilities – the Kent town of Margate, for instance, installed gas lighting in the streets. In Tom Parker's study, viewers can clearly see the plans he has for Sanditon in miniature in the model he has had made of the town: there is a pier, a lighthouse and several, as yet unbuilt, crescents.

However, Parker hasn't suggested a public garden, which was a vogue during the period. Pleasure gardens fell into two categories. The first were simply public parks. These were publicly funded and free to enter (several of these parks are still in existence along the south coast of England today). The second were gardens owned by private investors, which usually charged an entrance fee. They offered entertainment, such as bandstands and magicians, and were already popular in London. The most famous evocation of one such pleasure garden appears in William Makepeace Thackeray's *Vanity Fair*.

The popularity of gardens is not a huge surprise. Georgians were fascinated by botany. Among the bestsellers of the era were illustrated botanical texts, which were hugely expensive, and many of them had hand-tinted illustrations. Queen Charlotte herself helped found Kew Gardens, just outside London – and the public were keen to view interesting plants and attend lectures that explored the growing botanical sciences around plant life, including soil types and geology. The balmy weather along the south coast meant that many of these gardens flourished, although none of the private pleasure gardens with their lush entertainments are still in existence.

Above: Queen Charlotte.

Below left and above: Ryde,
Isle of Wight.

Other public facilities that might be developed included a 'promenade', or wide pavement area usually along the sea-front, where visitors could take a long walk in the healthy seaside air. Seaside piers were just about to come into fashion - a'chain pier' at Ryde on the Isle of Wight opened in 1814 – the first seaside pleasure pier in the world. Piers were important as a docking station for sailing or paddle boats (and later steamships). These would deposit visitors into the heart of a seaside town without them having to be carried off the boat individually or walk in wet sand up to the settlement. Gradually, though, piers became more than just a drop-off point and were built far wider, with room for fairground attractions, entertainment venues, ice-cream stalls and cafés, some stretching out to sea for over a mile – like the pier at Southend. As well as providing a place to disembark, these longer piers were seen as a way to take in as much sea air as possible. They remain a feature of the British seaside town to this day.

'By nine o'clock my uncle, aunt and I entered the Rooms and linked Miss Winstone on to us. Before tea it was rather a dull affair; but then the before tea did not last long, for there was only one dance, danced by four couple. Think of four couple, surrounded by about an hundred people, dancing in the Upper Rooms at Bath! After tea we cheered up; the breaking up of private parties sent some scores more to the ball, and though it was shockingly and inhumanly thin for this place, there were people enough to have made five or six very pretty Basingstoke assemblies.'

Jane Austen's description of an evening she spent at the
Bath Upper Rooms in May 1801, shortly after arriving in the city

Another important building in a seaside settlement was the town hall, which often included what were known as the 'assembly rooms' – where the balls in *Sanditon* take place. These public entertainment venues could be huge. The Assembly Rooms in Bath, opened in 1771, could accommodate 1,200 visitors at a single event. Commonly there were two events each week – everything from public talks, operas and concerts to balls and masques where, in addition to dancing, guests might eat, drink and play cards. When she lived in Bath between 1801 and 1805 Jane Austen attended dances in what at the time were called the 'Upper Rooms', because in the Georgian era there were also 'Lower Rooms', which accommodated even more social activity. The Bath Assembly Rooms are still in use today and the décor has not changed a great deal since Austen's visits: five impressive crystal chandeliers (each weighing as much as a small car) are suspended over the light, airy dancing space, which is 30 metres long, and there are a further three public rooms that were used for events during the Regency. Today, the Assembly Rooms are also home to a fashion museum. Used as a location in several Austen adaptations – including the film of *Northanger Abbey* in 1987, and two television productions of *Persuasion*, one filmed in 1994 starring Amanda Root as Anne Elliot and a second in 2006 starring Sally Hawkins. The Assembly Rooms also host an annual ball as part of the Jane Austen Festival, which takes place in September.

While visitors flocked to the seaside for health reasons, these resorts became large and important social centres with a vibrant life and community of their own. They thrived well into the Victorian era and beyond, attracting tourists from all social classes.

The Assembly Rooms, Bath.

BEHIND THE SCENES

Getting the Sanditon look

'There's something about Jane,' Grant Montgomery, production designer, says. 'She's different from any other writer. Everyone feels as if they know her.' Montgomery is a big Austen fan but he knew he wanted to do something different with the design for this special production. 'This novel was unique in her work. It was the first time she really talked about death and the first time she talked about business too. It was a departure and I thought, "How can I make this look different?" I came up with the idea of bringing James Bond to the Regency. I decided on drama. It was such a decadent period and "twee" Austen had been done, so I went for Wedgwood tones – something much darker than the traditional Austen production design.'

Montgomery heads up a team of around twenty craftsmen who built the sets. 'We had fourteen weeks to prepare and then we got building. The High Street took twelve weeks and Sanditon House took ten weeks,' he says. Grant's clever designs meant that some of the sets could be re-dressed and used on more than one occasion, like Lady Denham's black marble drawing room, which was restyled to become Sanditon's airy, white and gold assembly rooms and the location of the more vivid London ball featured later in the series. To pull this off, he explains,

required clear branding for each location. 'Lady Denham is a show-off. She's a snob. Her emblem was the snake and we put that on everything. The set had to reflect her character and she's all about power and dominance. Whereas Tom Parker is a businessman; he's founding Sanditon the brand so we put his "TP" logo onto as much as we could – everything from his carriage to the bathing wagons he has installed at the beach. The result is decadent and sexy – it's heightened reality.' To bring the coastal location into almost every shot, Montgomery made sure that Denham House contained a large collection of seaside paintings and sculptures. 'It's everywhere,' he says. 'In everything we could think of. Those tiny visual prompts are really important.'

Computer-generated imagery (CGI) was kept to a minimum so Montgomery and his team created sets that could easily cut to shots of a real beach. 'We made an archway – like an alleyway – at the end of the street scene and then built a portable arch, took it to the beach and shot through that. There is a little bit of CGI, which is used for details – like the row of bathing huts (the first one or two are real but the rest were added post-production) and for extra houses in Sanditon itself. Mostly, though, what you see is what was genuinely on set.'

Montgomery is enthusiastic about Sanditon as a place. He suggested building the model in Tom Parker's study and creating Parker's map – both of which were based on objects in John Soane's house in London. This was to give an authentic feel. 'We used a lot of real candlelight,' he enthuses. 'That's difficult to recreate and it has given the production a beautiful tone. It's like being there.' For Edward and Esther's house, he wanted to create something darker and sexier, designing Gothic door lintels and lush murals of naked ladies. 'It was very Byronic,' he admits. Right through the production, Montgomery's team inserted tiny details to add authenticity – a first edition of *Pride and Prejudice* in Diana Parker's house, for example. Or creating food that would have been prepared, like the calves' feet served at Lady Denham's house.

SIDNEY PARKER
Theo James

TOM:

My brother's merits are often slow to advertise themselves.

Charlotte spreads some of Tom's Gentleman's Relish on her toast.

CHARLOTTE:

Perhaps he is an acquired taste then, sir. Like anchovy paste?

TOM:

Ho ho. Well said, Charlotte! That's it exactly. Far too peppery for some. But altogether habit-forming once you get the hang of it!

– Episode 4

'Sidney Parker was about seven or eight and twenty, very good-looking with a decided air of ease and fashion and a lively countenance.'

SANDITON

Sidney Parker, played by Theo James

Tom Parker's younger brother, Sidney, is a successful businessman who has seen a lot of the world. He owns a warehouse in London and imports expensive commodities like sugar and coffee. Sidney comes to Sanditon to help his brother establish the resort, and Tom is relying on Sidney's connections and his business skills. During his time in Antigua he befriended Georgiana Lambe's father and became her guardian on his death. Sidney does not relish this role. He is a young man with his own life to lead and Georgiana's unhappiness and rebellion are beyond him. At first Sidney is exasperated by Charlotte Heywood's forthright nature, but he comes to admire her cool head in a crisis.

When did you learn to ride a horse? And did you realise at the time it would be so handy?

I learned to ride for another period drama some years ago . . . but I'm still terrible.

Are Regency clothes comfortable?

Men's Regency clothing tends to be very fitted, even skintight, so not entirely comfortable. But the clothing aids characterisation. It helps me remember to improve my terrible posture!

What's the difference between this kind of drama and acting in a thriller like *How It Ends*?

The period is extremely informative for your sense of character. Unlike filming something contemporary, there are historical and cultural anchors that are so different from the way we move and interact today. It means there's a wealth of detail to be explored and used as an actor.

What do you like about Sidney?

Sidney is an extremely complex character, consumed by both his arrogance and self-loathing. His love for his family pulls him back to Sanditon, but problematic events in his past have damaged and shaped him irrevocably. His hard exterior is matched by his fiery temper, but through Charlotte we begin to understand his true nature is, in fact, one of loyalty and love.

Sidney lives in a complicated world, doesn't he?

Regency England saw the expansion of British colonialism and its dominance as a global trading power. With it came a sense of culture and societal extravagance in the upper classes. Men particularly dressed well, held themselves with confidence and assurance. In London there was an ability to indulge in life's more hedonistic riches – sex, gambling, opium and alcohol. This, for me, cements elements of Sidney's character. He lives a wild, unrestrained life but part of him is repulsed by its frivolity.

Bristol

a

Bath

b

c

d

Exeter

Plymouth

a London ~ Bristol : 2 days
b London ~ Bath : 2 days
c London ~ Exeter : 3 days
d London ~ Plymouth : 4 days
e London ~ Margate : 2 days

LONDON

Margate

e

Fair weather journey times to popular
Georgian seaside resorts by coach from London.

Bad weather would have meant coaches
took even longer.

BEHIND THE SCENES

Ensuring authenticity

Dr Hannah Greig is based at the University of York and is an expert in eighteenth- and nineteenth-century British history. She has advised on several productions for film and TV and was involved with the *Sanditon* team from the early stages of the series, coming on board in spring 2018.

'I'm an on-call geek,' she says with a smile. Greig's job is to be available to everyone involved with the production, providing expert historical support for everything from story development to production design. 'The exciting thing with *Sanditon* was that Austen didn't finish the story, so that meant we had to look at what was going to happen after she put down her pen,' Greig explains.

Historical accuracy was hugely important in creating Sanditon as a seaside town. 'We're familiar with English seaside towns now, but we think of them as twee places of historical interest. In the Regency, these towns were brand new. They were edgy places and potentially exciting – the height of modernity,' Greig says. 'People were thrown together.' She worked closely with production designer Grant Montgomery, who also has a keen interest in history. 'He has a real eye for detail, which is what you need if you want to construct a convincing world from the past,' Greig enthuses.

As well as the script and the set, Greig's advice is

often sought about small details, which can have a huge impact on how the story comes across. She highlights the importance of ensuring that the way money is handled is authentic. 'How much does Tom Parker spend on his building project, for example? That sum has to be right and tie in with the rest of society around him. He's taking a huge risk,' she explains. 'The smallest question can point to something bigger. What does someone keep in their pocket? What would you see in the shop window as you went past? Who is in the street and is that appropriate at that time of the day?'

Greig is an Austen enthusiast who grew up reading *Emma* and *Pride and Prejudice*. 'We imagine the Regency through Austen's eyes from quite a young age. She has shaped the way we view this whole historical period,' she says. When it comes to bringing the carefully constructed scripts to life, however, the most important thing is adding the acting talent. Attending the script read-throughs, where the actors voice the words for the first time together in a studio, is one of her favourite parts of the job. 'It's a special moment when the story comes to life. You find out if the jokes really are funny. It's exciting – the interplay between the characters comes to the fore. It's like magic.'

· • • ·

Bathing costumes and wagons

CHARLOTTE: I hear you're an advocate for sea-bathing?

SIR EDWARD: I am. Miss Heywood, you must experience it! The bracing shock of the first plunge. And then the incomparable feeling of freedom and lightness, the ocean bearing you up when you give yourself to it fearlessly, the delicate play of the currents over your naked limbs – nothing can give such a sense of well-being!   *Episode 1*

One of the most keenly anticipated moments in *Sanditon* has definitely been the sea-bathing scene. Again, this has a clear grounding in history. At the seaside, women and men bathed in the sea for the perceived health benefits of the salt water as well as the 'fresh air' or 'ozone'. In larger towns they would bathe separately – in Brighton there were two distinct beaches in use right up until the 1930s, one for each gender. This meant, in practice, that people often chose to bathe in the nude. However, in smaller towns, such as Sanditon, those taking a skinny dip would opt either to do so away from prying eyes or to stay in a different section of the water. Women would almost always wear a bathing robe, if they were within view. These robes, which were like white cotton nightdresses, were also commonly used when taking a hot bath at home.

Bathing machines on the beach.

Women's daywear for the beach allowed hems to be a little higher than was usual in order to protect the fabric of the dresses from the sand and salt. Parasols and straw hats were also de rigueur for women at the seaside.

As seen in this production, contemporary illustrations show 'bathing wagons' or 'bathing machines'. These were huts on wheels that could be driven into the sea by a horse and driver to a depth that would allow the bather to open the door and get straight into the water, thus safeguarding their modesty. A canopy might be added at the back and could be lowered to provide a completely sequestered bathing area if required. The huts were used for changing out of day clothes and often a 'dipper' (for women) or 'bather' (for men) might be employed as a servant to help the swimmer to submerge.

Letters – keeping in touch

Lady Denham finishes reading a letter and throws it down on the table with a sigh

CLARA: Not bad news I hope, aunt?

LADY DENHAM: The Earl of Sussex is engaged. How dreadfully inconsiderate of him! *Episode 4*

Letters were the only way to keep in touch and the middle and upper classes wrote to each other frequently. There had been a public Royal Mail service in Britain since the 1630s and by the Regency period it was widespread and provided revenue to the government. The person receiving the letter would pay for delivery. Charges were set according to how far the letter had to travel and how many sheets of paper it contained – it was a relatively expensive service used only by the wealthy. Paper was also costly, so most people kept their letters as short as they could and wrote small. Some people 'cross-wrote' letters, which means that rather than use a second sheet of paper, they wrote their letter, turned the page 90 degrees and continued writing across the original text. An envelope would have been charged as a

'A love letter is an investment. It's such a vulnerable thing to send your emotions out into the world like that.'

Crystal Clarke, playing Georgiana Lambe

Above: A crossed letter.

Below: A Royal Mail coach providing a combined passenger and mail delivery service.

second sheet of paper, so most individual letters were penned on a single sheet, which was then folded and sealed using wax. If you could not afford to pay for your letter when it arrived, it would be kept for you at the post office. In London several private mail services operated as well as the 'penny post', which was paid in advance and meant that, at 1817 prices, the threepence flat fee charged per letter within the capital cost significantly less to deliver than elsewhere in the country.

Post was slow due to the poor state of the roads. It was common for a letter from London to Bath to take three days to arrive. In the early Regency period, deliveries were made by 'post boy' (usually a young boy travelling alone), but these shipments were frequently robbed by thieves on the roads and later mail coaches were established, which also carried passengers. These coaches were frequently overladen with

people – those with the cheapest tickets riding on top with their luggage and the mail bags. The mail coaches carried a guard dressed in red livery and armed with a blunderbuss musket. This hugely improved the safety of the mail.

Originally a 'stamp' wasn't a piece of paper stuck to the letter, but an inked mark that was applied at the post office – what today we would call a 'postmark'. There were no postcodes. House numbers were only just being introduced by the time of the Regency, so most letters were simply addressed to the person by name and, if the postman was lucky, there might be a street name. Many were addressed only to the recipient's town and might read: Mrs Smith, Eastbourne.

As well as operating within the UK, letters could be sent abroad – a single page to the West Indies cost twenty-two pence, more than most people earned in a day. Again, delivery was slow: the West Indies and America packet left only once a month and was subject to delays according to the weather.

If you were sending a letter or note locally outside London, it was almost always cheaper (and frequently quicker) to pay someone to deliver it for you on foot.

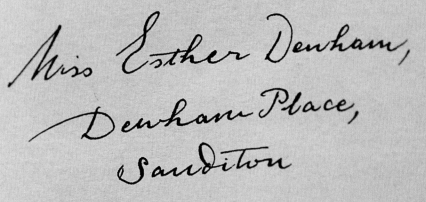

Miss Esther Denham,
Denham Place,
Sanditon

JAMES STRINGER
Leo Suter

OLD STRINGER:
My son is a foreman. It is not his place to be drawing up plans.

CHARLOTTE:
But might a man not elevate his position, Mr Stringer, if he is blessed with talent and prepared to work hard?

YOUNG STRINGER:
Aye, miss. Those are my feelings exactly.

OLD STRINGER:
I must beg to differ. You make the best of the hand you're dealt and it's a fool says otherwise.

OLD STRINGER:
You are the son of a mason. No use aiming for grouse when you should be shooting pigeons. Else you shall end up hungry.

– Episode 4

James Stringer, played by Leo Suter

Tom Parker's right-hand man, Young Stringer is the foreman of the Sanditon building project. He is ambitious, talented and hard-working – a real asset to Sanditon and the classic example of a working-class Regency man who could (perhaps, given his vision) rise in society – despite the fact his father is more comfortable when people know their place. He develops a crush on Charlotte Heywood, who is open, friendly and also engaged with the project – but Charlotte is the daughter of a gentleman.

James Stringer longs to be a self-made man. How much did you look into working-class life in the Regency when you took the role?
Olly, the director, recommended a couple of books and I read those to find out what life was like. Not easy. But that's what drew me to the script – it's exciting to play a working-class character in an Austen story. Stringer's world (his house, his job, his dog Hercules) stands as a contrast to the ball scenes and dinner parties.

What inspires you about Jane Austen's novels?
The characters are so funny and well observed. She writes young people so well and the honesty of young love.

Stringer's relationship with his father is touching and both characters are close on screen. How do you like working with Rob Jarvis, who plays Old Stringer?

He's a wonderful actor to work opposite and learn from. He's a really warm-hearted, decent man.

Do you enjoy playing a range of different historical characters, such as the prime minister's private secretary, Edward Drummond, in ITV's *Victoria* and the foreman Young Stringer in *Sanditon*?

It's a really exciting way to keep things fresh. These characters exist in similar eras, but at different ends of the socio-economic spectrum, so I get to explore how the other half live and have a foot in each camp.

You were a cricket fan when you were younger. Was it fun filming the cricket scenes?

I'm a fan and I play regularly too. When I saw the script, it put a smile on my face and I couldn't wait to bowl at Sidney and give him some 'chin music'.

Should James leave Sanditon for the bright lights of London? Would you?

Oh – the pull of the Big Smoke is huge. He's a man with aspirations after all and the rewards are great. That move would be emblematic for him of what you get when you work hard and succeed.

· • • • ·

Georgian roads and the uncomfortable business of travel

CHARLOTTE HEYWOOD is asleep. Squeezed in between her fellow passengers, she holds tight to her small bag of belongings as her head nods in rhythm with the coach. As the coach comes to an abrupt halt, Charlotte jerks awake. *Episode 6*

Travelling in Regency England was not an easy business. If you decided to go by road (and for longer journeys within the UK – going from, say, London to Edinburgh – a boat was frequently quicker), you were in for a long and probably uncomfortable journey. Roads were not always publicly owned and on a private road all coaches would be expected to pay a toll, or fee. These 'turnpike roads' were better maintained and improved travel times and comfort on the muddy and dangerous thoroughfares of the mid-eighteenth century, but they also increased travel costs.

The rich used their own carriages, which were manned

'If I went back to the Regency, I'd miss travelling in a car. Carriages are too bouncy – a bit like a badly sprung taxi. On TV you look fine getting out but in real life you'd be wrecked by the time you'd got from London to Bath.'

Anne Reid, playing Lady Denham

by their personal staff, often dressed in the family livery. Travelling this way meant you could manage the journey – stopping whenever and wherever you wanted. While the rich sometimes used coaching inns, they were more likely to

Tourists loading luggage onto a carriage as they leave their lodging house in Scarborough, 1813.

stop (particularly overnight) and stay with friends en route. Gentlemen frequently travelled on horseback and alone. Most people, however, booked on to either stagecoaches or mail coaches, which meant riding with unknown fellow travellers in close proximity. In an era when good personal hygiene was not a given, this could be extremely unpleasant. It also meant that you might get stuck next to a chatterbox! Passengers travelled with copious luggage – it was not un-heard of for live animals (hunting dogs, for example) to be sent by coach. Corpses might also be transported, either for burial or for dissection at medical schools.

Progress on the roads was slow, with overloaded coaches too heavy for the horses, going even more slowly. Progress was also dependent on the weather. If it was wet, for example, the road would become muddy and the horses would not be able to go as fast. If you were unlucky, you might find yourself travelling at a pace not much above walking speed – perhaps 4 miles an hour. Mail coaches only used the better roads (they dropped the route if the road became less passable) and also tended to carry fewer passengers in lighter coaches, which meant they travelled, on average, at around 9 miles per hour. Other traffic was required to get out of the way for mail coaches and this also made them faster. Tickets cost 2d (pence) per mile if you were travelling on the outside of the coach and between 4d and 5d per mile for inside – a not inconsiderable sum if you were going any distance, especially given the level of discomfort.

Journeys lurched between roadside inns where the horses were fed, watered and sometimes changed. Coaches often ran to a stringent timetable, so stops were kept to a minimum. Travellers had to be vigilant if they got off a coach to get something to eat, stretch their legs or go to the toilet (which meant simply using a chamber pot inside the inn). The coachman would have no qualms about leaving without passengers who did not fall in with the timetable and would do so with their luggage still on board.

Fossils and the Jurassic Coast

Fossil hunting was a common pastime for the middle-class Georgian gentleman and even some ladies. Fossil collections were the perfect additions to a 'cabinet of curiosities' – private collections that might be housed in a glass-fronted case or even take up a whole room. Cabinets commonly contained geological finds and relics, as well as fossils and other items of interest – exactly the kind of thing you might find in a gentleman's study, like Tom Parker's.

The biggest talent in fossil collecting in the Regency era was Mary Anning. Anning was born into a poor family in Lyme Regis in Dorset. Lyme Regis lies on what is now known as the Jurassic Coast – a rich seam of ammonites and belemnite fossils that runs along the coastline. Self-taught in geology and anatomy, as a child Mary began selling her finds after her father died to help support her family.

In 1811, at the age of twelve, she meticulously excavated a 5.2-metre skeleton of a 200-million-year-old marine reptile after her brother found the skull. This was an extraordinary feat and at the time (several years before Charles Darwin's *On the Origin of Species*) it proved impossible to identify the skeleton. For decades, wild theories abounded about Mary's 'sea crocodile' and where it had come from. Anning then went on to uncover several other groundbreaking fossils,

Above: English fossil collector Mary Anning with her dog Tiny.

selling her finds to male scientists who often did not credit her when they wrote about 'their' discoveries. The work was dangerous: fossils were often exposed as a result of landslides in bad weather – her dog, Tray, was killed in one and Mary was lucky to escape with her life. She frequently had to work quickly before the fossils were washed away. She found the first pterodactyl discovered outside Germany (called 'pterosaur' at the time) and pioneered the study of coprolites (or fossilised faeces). Museums and public collections sprang up across Britain and public interest in fossil discoveries was huge.

Mary was paid poorly, though her work was highly valued by many. Her childhood friend, Henry de la Beche, made prints of some of her finds to raise money to help support her. She died aged only forty-seven, in poverty. Today, Mary Anning's fossils are housed in major collections around the world, including the Natural History Museum in London. It is said that the children's tongue-twister 'She sells seashells by the seashore' was written about her.

Right: 'Ancient Dorset' painted in 1830 by Henry De La Beche based on fossils found by Mary Anning.

Mary Anning's
Fossil Depot,
Lyme Regis.

Fossil shops were popular in seaside towns of the period. Anning herself opened one in Lyme Regis. Specimens, as well as geological finds, were seen as great mementos to take home from a holiday by the sea. Jane Austen was well aware of this Regency vogue – she visited Lyme Regis in 1804 (and went on to feature it in her novel *Persuasion*).

'... the remarkable situation of the town, the principal street almost hurrying into the water, the walk to the Cobb, skirting round the pleasant little bay, which, in the season, is animated with bathing machines and company; the Cobb itself, its old wonders and new improvements, with the very beautiful line of cliffs, stretching out to the east of the town, are what the stranger's eye will seek; and a very strange stranger it must be who does not see charms in the immediate environs of Lyme, to make him wish to know it better.'

Persuasion

3
STORY of SANDITON

⚜

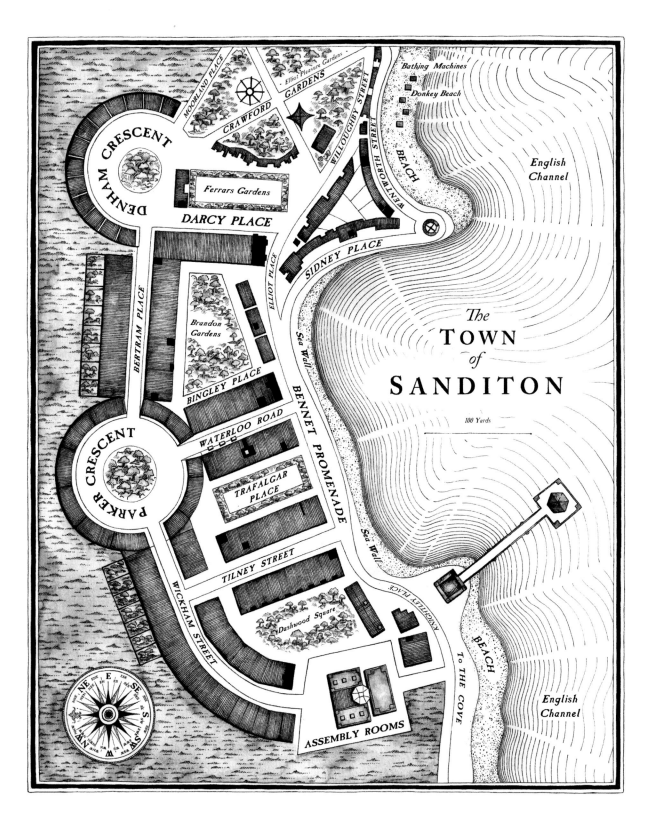

CHARLOTTE: Mr Crowe, how do you rate Sanditon's chances of succeeding?

CROWE: Pretty slim, at present, ma'am. Can't hold a candle to Brighton, or Bath – not enough here to tempt a man of fashion – or a lady.   *Episode 2*

ARTHUR: First-class medical care is what will distinguish the fashionable resort of the future from the second-rate.   *Episode 2*

MISS LAMBE: This is such a blessed relief from life in dull, dreary old Sanditon. How I wish we could escape it altogether.

CHARLOTTE: Come, Georgiana. Sanditon is not as bad as all that. As a matter of fact, I am exceedingly fond of the place.   *Episode 4*

WHEN JANE AUSTEN sat down to write *Sanditon* in 1817, we don't know what she had in mind for the story, but we do know that the bond between Tom, Sidney and Arthur Parker was key in her mind. In her eleven-chapter opening, originally called *The Brothers*, we are introduced to all three Parker men – Tom, the visionary; Sidney, the fixer; and Arthur, the hypochondriac. We also meet Charlotte and the Denham clan – cruel Lady Denham holding the prospect of inheritance over her nieces and nephew, Clara, Esther and Edward. Edward is drawn particularly clearly: good-looking and out to make trouble, he enjoys a conquest and in the opening of the book is clearly attracted to both Charlotte and Clara – just to see if he can succeed. Georgiana Lambe, the heiress from the West Indies, also features, although only briefly towards the end of the original text when she arrives in the resort. She is the only black character Jane Austen ever wrote and she hardly gets to speak – though there is no question her character would have developed over the course of the book had Austen lived to finish it. Black characters in novels of this period are unusual (though not unheard of) and creating Georgiana was a bold move by Austen, who supported the abolition of slavery. Black heirs and heiresses (often the illegitimate children of plantation owners) came to Britain to be educated and/or launched into society with a view to making a good marriage.

'Sanditon is a little world of its own! For Clara it is a paradise away from the troubles of her childhood.'

Lily Sacofsky, playing
Clara Brereton

Jane herself had spent a considerable amount of time on the south coast of England in seaside towns. After her father retired in 1801, the Austen family spent the summers visiting friends on the coast at Worthing, Bognor Regis, Eastbourne and Totnes, all of which were developing rapidly at the time; investors in the local economy hoped that they would become fashionable seaside resorts to rival Brighton. Austen's experiences over the course of these visits must have inspired *Sanditon*, and the newly built terraces with houses for hire, seaside libraries and local shops that she draws in the opening chapters are based on these.

Austen's last, unfinished novel, however, was almost completely unknown outside her family and a few academics who had had access to her papers, until it was published in 1925 by the Clarendon Press, an imprint of Oxford University Press. Robert Chapman, editor at the press, was fascinated by Jane Austen's work and produced a series of new editions and a collected works during the 1920s. It is believed that Chapman's wife, Katherine Metcalfe, who was an English tutor at Somerville College, Oxford, worked closely with him, although she was not credited for her contribution. Katherine's handwriting is commonly found all over Chapman's notes for his Austen editions. Since Chapman's edition of the *Sanditon* fragment, a few writers have written forward from her promising start, but the story has never been dramatised for television or feature film. This production completes the vibrant world that Austen started to create – or as Executive Producer Belinda Campbell puts it: '*Sanditon*'s themes of class divide, ambition, power play and matters of the heart are as relevant today as they were in the early nineteenth century.'

'*Andrew Davies is brilliant at setting up characters. You know who people are from the moment you meet them. His writing is a masterclass in economy.*'

Nick Lambon,
story producer

As Austen's final novel, *Sanditon* is her most 'modern' work and it's interesting she chose to set it in a vibrant, newly built town that would have been considered cutting edge at the time. Andrew Davies, the screenwriter who conceived *Sanditon*, wanted to retain that atmosphere of the new and, sometimes, slightly dangerous. The famous lake scene in Davies' 1995 TV adaptation of *Pride and Prejudice* was originally written with Mr Darcy bathing nude. However, this was vetoed by the producer, who felt that Darcy emerging soaking wet in breeches and a shirt was sexier! In *Sanditon*, however, Davies gets his way, with several nude bathing scenes, which are also more authentic for male seabathing of the time. Austen never wrote about downmarket or dangerous locations in her work. This might be because Jane knew little about those kinds of places – she was brought up in a manse, after all. However, they certainly existed in abundance. This production takes Austen's world and extends it into the wider historical context of Regency England, a fascinating, rambunctious and contradictory place.

Ultimately, though, it's always the characters, with their foibles and concerns, hopes and fears, that touch readers. The characters in *Sanditon*, on ice after Austen's death for over 200 years, are brought startlingly to life in this production – the work of writers, producers, directors, actors, set designers, wardrobe and make-up coming together to tell the compelling story Austen wanted to tell and providing a link between her world and our own – a bridge from history to today.

'The Parker family are unique and wonderful; the three Parker brothers are all very different – Tom is a dreamer and the pioneer behind Sanditon, Sidney is handsome and unpredictable, and Arthur, in addition to his love of food and wine, is a joyful bundle of contradictions.'

Turlough Convery, playing Arthur Parker

CAST

DRAMATIS PERSONAE

Charlotte Heywood:
Rose Williams

Lady Denham:
Anne Reid

Sidney Parker:
Theo James

Georgiana Lambe:
Crystal Clarke

Sir Edward Denham:
Jack Fox

Esther Denham:
Charlotte Spencer

Clara Brereton:
Lily Sacofsky

Tom Parker:
Kris Marshall

Mary Parker:
Kate Ashfield

Arthur Parker:
Turlough Convery

James Stringer:
Leo Suter

Otis Molyneux:
Jyuddah Jaymes

Diana Parker:
Alexandra Roach

Mrs Griffiths:
Elizabeth Berrington

Mr Heywood:
Adrian Rawlins

Lord Babington:
Mark Stanley

Mr Crowe:
Matthew Needham

Mr Hankins:
Kevin Eldon

Dr Fuchs:
Adrian Scarborough

BEHIND THE SCENES

Capturing the spirit of Jane Austen

Dr Paula Byrne is a biographer, novelist and Jane Austen consultant to the *Sanditon* series. She is well aware of the responsibility of having to 'live up to' Jane Austen's legacy. 'With Austen, of all authors, readers feel they are in a complicit, intimate relationship. It's the craft of her writing that makes us feel involved,' she says. 'We refer to her as "Jane", unlike fans of Dickens or Trollope, who never use the author's first name.'

With an unfinished novel like *Sanditon* nobody knows what Austen intended. Reading scripts in advance of shooting and attending on set, it's her job to ensure that what appears on screen feels consistent with the Austen canon. That isn't always about historical detail – her favourite Austen adaptation (so far) is the 1995 romantic comedy, *Clueless*, starring Alicia Silverstone and set in 1990s California, which is loosely based on Austen's *Emma*. 'She would have loved it,' Byrne enthuses. 'It's so funny – very satirical.'

However, some of the devil is in the detail. Initially, producers planning the bathing scenes had placed female characters as well as male ones naked in the water. Byrne pointed out this inaccuracy – women would have bathed

'Look at Jane Austen. Her characters derive in a reasonably straight line from fairy tales.'

Andrew Davies, screenwriter

wearing turbans and muslin shifts. 'The scene originally also had men and women far too close together,' she says. 'In the end the producers moved them to opposite ends of the beach. It was a small detail but important to strike the right tone. It's the kind of thing that might have made Austen fans lose faith in the production.'

Byrne is a huge *Sanditon* fan, spotting a freshness in the first chapters of the book and hailing it as a departure from the 'drawing room', taking Austen's characters into the emerging world of the Regency seaside where, unlike the gentry she often places centre stage, the main characters are committed to making money and are not necessarily from the upper echelons of Georgian society. 'The chapters we have are very immediate. I felt it was important to keep the drama of Austen's opening – the Parkers' carriage accident – which sets the whole story off. I'm convinced, had she finished it, the novel would have shown a development in her storytelling. Many Austen enthusiasts hail *Persuasion* as Austen's swansong – and cite the autumnal, mournful feel of the novel as evidence that she knew she was dying, but *Sanditon* belies that idea. It's the last thing she wrote and it's vital.'

Byrne's favourite aspect of the story is the way it echoes one of Austen's favourite authors, Richardson, whose most famous character, Pamela, was a servant girl. Another is the way it echoes Austen's own life. 'Austen's cousin, Eliza, took her young son, Hastings, to the seaside because he was ill in the late 1790s,' she says. 'She wrote to Jane, enthusing about the health benefits. In a way the seaside democratised expensive spa towns – sea bathing was free. The sea air was free. Improving roads made access easier. It might not have been for the poor but there was a "raffish", middle-class aspect to these seaside towns, as well as a whole movement that tied in with the Romanticism prevalent in the period – all about the bounty and beauty of nature.'

OTHER ADAPTATIONS
OF THE BOOK

· · · ·

1845: Austen's niece, Anna Austen Lefroy, attempts to finish Sanditon, but abandons the project.

1975: Australian journalist Marie Dobbs publishes a completion of the novel, marketing it as 'by Jane Austen and another lady'.

2000: Julie Barrett, who wrote other continuations of Jane Austen stories, publishes her completion of Sanditon.

2002: D. J. Eden publishes her completion of the novel.

2008: The twenty-first book in the Dalziel and Pascoe series by Reginald Hill, A Cure for All Diseases, uses Sanditon as inspiration (setting the action in the Yorkshire town of Sandytown).

2011: Anne Toledo, a university professor of English literature living in Italy, publishes her version, titled A Return to Sanditon.

2011: Austen expert, Donald Measham, writes Jane Austen out of the Blue, his reimagining of Sanditon, which references Austen in the text.

2013: Web series Welcome to Sanditon, set in present-day California, is broadcast.

2014: Two short Sanditon-based documentaries by Hampshire enthusiast Chris Brindle are released.

History of the novel: where the stories come from

The word 'novel' derives from the Italian *novella,* which was coined in the medieval period to denote a short fictional story. The term was first used in the early eighteenth century, and novels were available in English for about a hundred years before Jane Austen was first published. The term referred to longer-form fiction, so anything over about 50,000 words. As a literary form, though, the novel was not taken seriously. Because books were hugely expensive to produce in the early era of the printing press, precedence was given to non-fiction titles, which were considered more educational and therefore more important. For most people, the art of storytelling principally came in the form of drama or performance. This is because the majority of the population was illiterate. Poetry was also more highly valued than the novel – in part because of its capacity to be performed and also because of the more stringent stylistic rules around its composition and the perceived skill in writing it.

The first book to be widely recognised as a novel was *Don Quixote* by Miguel de Cervantes (published in Spanish in 1605 and shortly after translated into English). It took over a century before the first novel actually written in English

'It's been such fun to develop Jane Austen's fragment into a series – now I'm eager to see our exceptional cast bring Sanditon *to life.'*

Andrew Davies,
screenwriter

appeared, widely agreed to be *Robinson Crusoe* by Daniel Defoe, which hit the bookshelves in 1719. Defoe went on to write *Moll Flanders* in 1722 and *Roxana* in 1724. These early

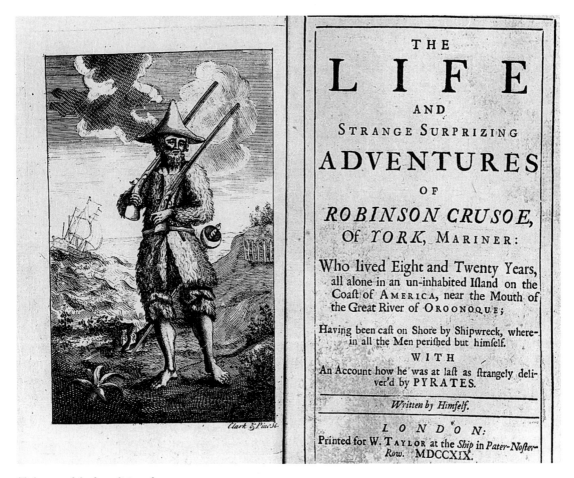

Title page of the first edition of Robinson Crusoe, 1719.

novels were groundbreaking – nobody had written for a popular audience about the inner life of fictional characters in prose, and certainly not the inner lives and thoughts of ordinary people. Robinson Crusoe, a shipwrecked sailor, the unfortunate Moll Flanders who falls from grace and Roxana – a courtesan – were nothing like the worthy, aristocratic characters written about in non-fiction works of the period.

Defoe was at pains to present his stories as if they were true, inserting chapter titles like 'The True History of . . .' and 'The Legend of . . .' Forms such as the epistolary novel (like Jane Austen's early work *Susan*) also suggested the fiction was real, providing evidence – in this case actual letters between the characters. While there were, in international literature, some innovative fictional works before the eighteenth century (including in English *Le Morte d'Arthur* by Thomas Malory – which was never called a novel in its own time), Defoe's novels were the first books written in English for an English audience that had a widespread impact. It was a long time before genre fiction began to emerge, such as fantasy stories or crime books.

Novels became hugely popular relatively quickly. In the Regency period, the readers of novels (as today) were mostly female. And, in fact, some women, who wanted to be taken seriously, refused to read novels at all. When Maria Graham, travel writer and mathematician, was sent a copy of *Emma* by her publisher, John Murray, she chided him in a letter, saying she didn't have time to read such 'nonsense'. Austen was therefore at the forefront of this relatively new literary form and her writing approach was highly experimental – especially in her early work as a young lady, which includes prose stories, short plays and poems.

BEHIND THE SCENES

Sanditon completed

Writer Kate Riordan was approached in February 2018 to write *Sanditon* the novel. A former journalist who now writes historical novels, she immediately wanted the job. 'I had to write a 2,000-word sample,' she explains, 'along with the other writers who were in the running. I was nervous but I really enjoyed getting my ideas down on paper. I knew it was going to be a challenge as well as a huge responsibility, but I really wanted to do it.'

The novel was commissioned to be 80,000 words, which had to be delivered by May 2019, while the series was still filming. Riordan wrote it between her home in England and on holiday in France for a month. 'It was 10,000 words a week – quite the pace,' she admits, 'but I had the framework of Andrew Davies' wonderful scripts to work to, and all the dialogue.'

A long-time Austen fan, Riordan read her first Jane Austen novel, *Pride and Prejudice*, after watching Andrew Davies' 1995 adaptation at the age of fourteen. Her mother was an English teacher but, Riordan says, she still found the language of the book daunting and the TV adaptation provided an access point. 'I realised how funny Austen is. I love her odious Mr Collins and snobby Catherine de Bourgh. In *Sanditon*, the close cousins of these characters

'I learned to be a better writer through having things performed.'

Andrew Davies,
screenwriter

– the naive vicar and snobby Lady Denham – provide the same story function. I want Jane's natural sardonic wit to come through.'

To prepare, as well as analysing the scripts and visiting the set, Riordan read Georgette Heyer. 'Austen wasn't an historical writer – she was a contemporary one,' she enthuses. 'That means that she never felt the need to explain or describe the world because she could assume it. Heyer is wonderful at filling that gap for a contemporary reader – she gives a huge amount of fascinating historical detail that makes you feel that you are really there. I also worked hard to immerse myself in the language of the period. The

choice of a single word can make a big difference. Saying "excessively" instead of "very" places the reader firmly in the Regency, as does taking a slightly formal tone – women really did refer to their husbands using their title. It takes a light touch, but finding the right narrative voice makes all the difference.'

In creating *Sanditon*, she says, the main thing is that none of the details jar. 'Writing historical fiction, everything is there to trip you up – all it takes is one slip and you lose your reader. So, the main thing is not to break that fourth wall, to bring the reader with you into this seaside world with all its grit and magic. It has been hard work writing the book so quickly but, strangely, I could easily have made it longer. The biggest challenge was fitting everything in and capturing the richness of what the production team have created.'

THE WATSONS

At only 18,000 words long and with a mere five chapters, the other unfinished novel by Jane Austen, *The Watsons*, tells the story of a widowed clergyman and his four daughters. Austen started writing the book in Bath in 1803, but abandoned it after her father's death in 1805. As far as we know, it is the only writing project she undertook while living in the city. Jane discussed the novel with her sister, Cassandra, and told her that Mr Watson, who is gravely ill at the beginning of the story, was going to die. The rest of the story centres around Emma Watson, who, faced with financial difficulties on the marriage of her wealthy aunt (with whom she had been living), returns to her down-at-heel family in Surrey. Marriage for the four Watson girls (or at least one of them) is the theme of the book and in that it is a close cousin to *Pride and Prejudice*; but, although they attend balls and other social engagements, the Watsons are considerably worse off than the Bennet girls. It may be that Austen's real-life penury and the illness and subsequent death of her own father came too close to this fiction and she did not have the heart to complete it. However, as with *Sanditon*, several writers have subsequently tried to do so.

On 14 July 2011, Sotheby's auction house sold Austen's original manuscript of *The Watsons*. It was bought by the Bodleian Library in Oxford for £850,000.

History of the Library

Books were expensive in the Regency period and a library was a big investment for a gentleman to make. Books were bought with 'chap' (buff) covers and bound (usually in leather) according to a gentleman's taste, so that, for the wealthy, a whole library might contain books with exactly the same covers, liveried to match, just like their staff. Austen's access to private libraries with a range of books to read was a huge privilege – ordinary people would commonly only have a family Bible.

John Murray's early editions of Austen's own work sold for fifteen shillings each – more than most people in this era would spend in a week on food, so it was an item destined for a gentleman (or a lady). There was only one public library in the UK in the era in which *Sanditon* is set – the Chetham's Library in Manchester, which was founded by a wealthy donor in 1653 and was available to all.

However, in 1741 a group of miners from Leadhills in Lanarkshire set up the UK's first subscription library. Subscription libraries were also known as 'proprietors' libraries' and members paid an annual fee (and sometimes a joining fee) to fund the buying of books. In the case of the miners, they paid 15d (pence) to join and 10d per year to take part – a not inconsiderable amount given most miners could only hope to earn around twenty pounds a year. It was a great idea, which allowed ordinary people access to books, and subscription libraries began to spring up all over the UK. Some

'I am no indiscriminate novel reader. The mere trash of the common circulating library I hold in the highest contempt.'

Sanditon: Continued and Completed by Another Lady, Jane Austen and Marie Dobbs

'The library, of course, afforded everything: all the useless things in the world that could not be done without.'

Sanditon

were working-class organisations, like the Leadhills library; while others became a social focus for those who could have afforded books – these were considerably more expensive to join. Bromley House Library in Nottingham was founded in 1816 and cost five guineas to join plus a two-guinea annual fee – around four or five months' wages for a working man, well out of the reach of the majority. The Literary and Philosophical Society, in Newcastle, cost one guinea a year when the library opened in 1793. Private libraries were run by their members who chose which books they wanted to buy. This meant that their collections varied hugely; they often focused on particular areas of interest and might include other items to share – such as scientific instruments.

These were distinct from 'circulating' libraries, which also operated on a subscription basis but were commercial concerns. There were around 200 circulating libraries in the UK at the beginning of the nineteenth century. These libraries concentrated on popular books and were more likely to have collections of novels to read. They were especially popular in holiday or seaside towns, where visitors wanted to read without having to bring large (and heavy) books in their luggage. Circulating libraries often had souvenir shops that sold trinkets and had musical instruments and sheet music for hire.

The foundation of the modern library system, free to join and free to use, resulted from the 1850 Public Libraries Act – more than thirty years after *Sanditon* – and many circulating and subscription libraries became free during this era, as book prices decreased and newspapers became more affordable and easier to distribute around the country because of the expanding railway network. However, there are still some subscription libraries in the UK and, with the defunding of public libraries in recent years, these are now on the rise.

TOM PARKER
Kris Marshall

MARY PARKER:
My husband has two wives, Charlotte – myself and Sanditon; and I'd hesitate to say which of us he cares for most.

ESTHER:
Mr Tom Parker is a monomaniac who is well on the way to ruining himself and his family with his crazy schemes.

CHARLOTTE:
You don't really think that? I think his ideas are admirable.

ESTHER:
Wait till he bankrupts himself. I have nothing against his wife; indeed, I feel very sorry for her.

– Episode 1

Tom Parker,
played by Kris Marshall

Tom Parker is a man with a dream: he wants Sanditon to be a success – the ultimate fashionable Regency holiday destination. He is a kind-hearted and enthusiastic person willing to accept anyone, regardless of their background. His long-suffering wife, Mary, supports his obsession. Tom has sunk most of his personal funds into the project and now, if it fails, he will become bankrupt. His boundless energy and open heart make him an attractive character – someone to root for.

Tom Parker is obsessed. Did you enjoy playing him?

He's a visionary, trying to make the world a better place and leave a legacy. But he's human and flawed. Great fun.

You were born and brought up in Bath. Is Jane Austen second nature to you?

You'd think so! But until this job I'd never read any!

What did you learn on the set of *Sanditon* that you didn't know before?

That it's hard to sit in a chair in breeches . . .

How do you assess Tom's relationship with his wife Mary?

Strong, cool, progressive, equal yet ultimately tested.

How did you feel about dressing up in period costume?

As a tall man, I know that cut is everything. And they had beautifully cut clothes. Even if I have to jump from a second-floor window each morning to get into them!

So, is holidaying at the British seaside better than, say, the Caribbean? Because you'd know . . . after *Death in Paradise*.

There's no contest. Bognor every time!

'For my character, Sanditon is a lifetime vision . . . a Regency panacea. It cannot and will not fail.'

KRIS MARSHALL, PLAYING TOM PARKER

BEHIND THE SCENES

Shaping the story

The scriptwriting process for *Sanditon* started over a year before the cameras rolled. Before putting pen to paper, the team came together to work out the story. Nick Lambon, story producer for the show, says, 'It was exciting because Austen had only written a few chapters, so that was different to other adaptations everyone had worked on. At the start we spent a long time figuring out which bits to keep from Austen's original story and, after that, where we would take the series.' The team quickly decided that a second Parker sister in the original novel served the same story function as Diana Parker and it was decided to merge the two characters.

'Sanditon is a character, just like Broadchurch was a character.'

Paula Byrne,
Jane Austen consultant

The episodes were written by three different writers – four episodes by Andrew Davies, three by Justin Young and one by Andrea Gibb. As story producer, Nick was responsible for making sure that the characters and storylines stayed consistent. 'The tone and vision were set by Andrew Davies,' he says. 'We all followed his lead.'

Making sure that the writers were on the same page was not Nick's only task; he also worked closely with the rest of the production team to ensure what was written was achievable on screen and could be filmed within budget. 'We're always moving things around to get the

'The script is a blueprint for the production to follow. It's not only dialogue. It speaks to the whole team.'

Nick Lambon,
story producer

right balance of exterior and interior locations and make sure we are showing the audience as much of Sanditon as possible. Originally, the cricket match that forms a big part of Episode 5 was on a more traditional cricket field, but we came to the conclusion that it would work better set by the sea. Putting it on the beach felt absolutely right,' he says. 'All the way through it's been a priority to take advantage of the sea views.' Filming outside has its own issues, however. Production staff had to work hard to keep actors warm – especially during the naked bathing scenes!

It was also Nick's job to make sure the characters worked together. 'The way Andrew wrote the pineapple lunch in Episode 2 made us realise that it's more fun when our characters cross over into each other's stories,' he explains. 'So, when it came to Dr Fuchs' medical demonstration in Episode 3, we went through a number of iterations before the final version. At one stage, we moved the event to Trafalgar House and there was also a version that just had Esther, Clara, Edward and Lady Denham. But Fuchs is so much fun we felt we wanted as many of our characters there as possible. Sanditon House was the only place big enough for such a huge gathering and we moved it there.' He continues: 'The challenge and excitement is how to complete a Jane Austen novel. It was possible with this production to surprise the audience. In *Pride and Prejudice* everyone knows what is going to happen. But not with *Sanditon* because Austen didn't complete it. We wanted to make sure the story felt alive – it might be historical but it's anything but twee. We just hope audiences love it as much as we do.'

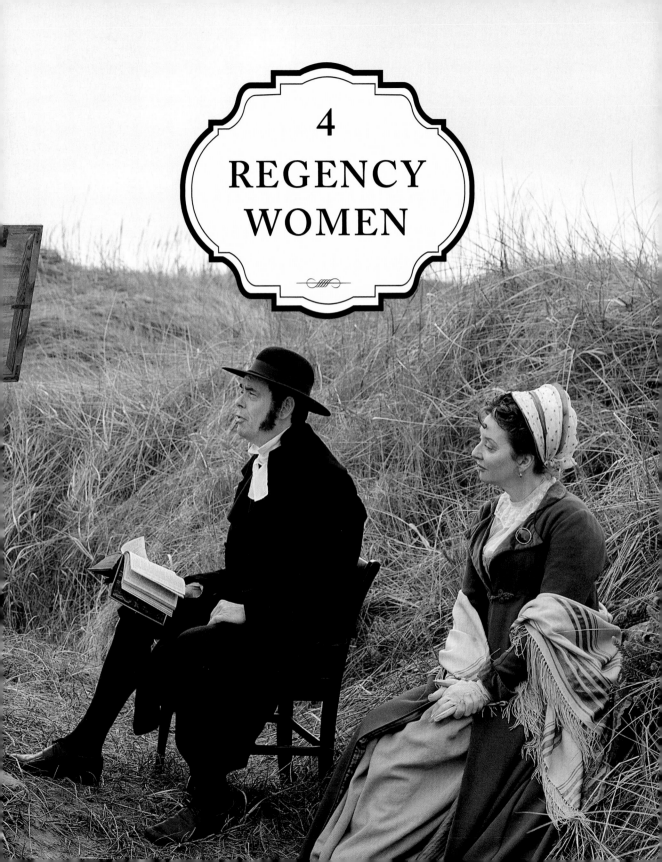

4
REGENCY WOMEN

LADY DENHAM: Love? Love? LOVE!
What does love have to do with anything?
Marriage is a business arrangement,
nothing more. *Episode 5*

T HE LIVES OF women in the Regency period were defined by their social position. Girls born into privileged upper- and middle-class families were groomed to marry well and advance the fortunes of their family. In 1814, just five years before *Sanditon* is set, the population of the UK contained only about 2,500 people who had been born into the high aristocracy and upper echelons of the Church. About half that number were women. On the next rung were the families of knights, baronets and monied country gentlemen, and this far larger group added just under a quarter of a million people to the population. Over a million people made up the group below that – clergy, doctors, lawyers, bankers, industrialists and those who had a moderate to good income. Jane Austen's characters are largely drawn from these more prosperous sectors of society and her stories centre around women (and their families) trying to advance their positions within this sphere. This was not a matter of historical interest for Jane – this was her real life. She lived as one of the roughly half a million women in the lowest rung of the class ladder outlined here and she was writing about issues that genuinely affected her life. The more than 16 million people living below Jane's station – working as servants, farm labourers, shopkeepers, craftspeople or those at the very bottom of society surviving in poverty – feature only fleetingly in Austen's stories, as they would have done in her life.

Women born into privilege, in any of the three upper groups, were not expected to work. In fact, if a woman chose to undertake some kind of paid profession, it was seen as a failing, as if her father, husband or other male relations could not afford to keep her. A woman's 'job' was to bear her husband (and his family) heirs, manage the household and help to fulfil and advance the family's social status. This might mean organising events like dances and making social calls to build the family's influence. Women's lives were protected – moving from their family home to their husband's home when they married, visiting people of the same social class (or, with luck, higher than their own), attending church and perhaps undertaking charity work. Jane Austen and her sister, for example, voluntarily taught poor children to read when they settled at Chawton towards the end of her life, establishing the Austens as benefactors – a worthy endeavour which would have brought social credit to their name.

Above: An engraving of three young women playing music and embroidering by Henry William Bunbury.

· · · ·

Education

A girl's education was usually different from that of her brothers. There was no compulsory legislation to regulate what children were taught, and, although most upper-class women learned to read and write, this depended on the priorities of their parents. Girls were taught primarily domestic and social skills – needlework, music, dancing, drawing/painting, household management and sometimes languages (particularly conversation), such as French and German. In the main women were discouraged from learning about politics, economics and science (except for botany) because these were considered 'male subjects'. Formal higher education was not open to women in the Regency period and no female students were accepted into university.

However, a few wealthy women, with supportive families, studied privately and excelled at these subjects. As a result these women lived more exciting and adventurous lives than the majority of their sisters. Rose Blaze de Bury (1813–1894), who was said to be the illegitimate daughter of Whig MP Lord Brougham, was born in Oban, Scotland, during the Regency. Rose received an excellent education and went on to become a hugely influential travel writer and economic adviser. When she lived in Paris, she set up a literary salon and wrote several novels, including one set against the backdrop of the French Revolution, *Mildred Vernon: A Tale of Parisian Life in the Last Days of the Monarchy.* She also drafted an economic plan for Austria in the 1850s and was key to the establishment of an Anglo-Austrian bank. Rose's correspondents included the Prussian statesman Otto von Bismarck. Also of note is Maria Graham (1785–1842), an English travel writer who published books about India, France, Chile and Brazil and who, while living in Chile in the 1820s, developed a mathematical formula to measure earthquakes. These women, though, were the exception rather than the rule, and both faced resistance to their work. When Maria Graham attempted to submit her mathematical equation to the Royal Society in London she was refused because of her gender, and it was only when Charles Darwin took up her case that she finally got to present her (entirely correct and groundbreaking) theory, which forms the basis of how we measure earthquakes today.

· • • ·

Launching a lady into society

It was up to the family when a young woman could be launched into society – usually this happened between the ages of fifteen and eighteen and was known as 'coming out'. Girls might 'come out' in their home town or go to London or Bath to experience the 'season', where they would stand a chance of meeting a far broader range of potential husbands. 'Being out' meant a young lady was allowed to attend public social engagements like dinner parties, dances and balls, and could be introduced into a wider social circle than they had enjoyed growing up. It signalled an end to childhood. Commonly, as mentioned in *Pride and Prejudice*, sisters were often not permitted to be 'out' simultaneously – giving an older sister time to find a husband before a younger one was launched into her own search. After the Regency and into the Victorian era, the term evolved and the practice of introducing young ladies at court also became known as 'coming out'. These women were referred to as 'debutantes', but in the Regency era coming out was not yet associated with life at court.

MRS GRIFFITHS: I am afraid it is out of the question! Picnics are the preserve of farmhands and savages!

CHARLOTTE: Forgive me, Mrs Griffiths, but I cannot entirely see the danger in eating out of doors.

MRS GRIFFITHS: It is an invitation to licentiousness! For a lady to be seated on the ground while eating – in full view of anyone who cares to pass! That is not just undignified, Miss Heywood, it is ungodly! *Episode 4*

Once out, most middle- and upper-class girls lived according to stifling rules that laid out what was appropriate. This 'etiquette' was part of their day-to-day lives and most never questioned it. The rules were designed to keep them safe from gossip, which might damage their reputation prior to marriage. Single women (even heiresses to large fortunes), for example, could not live or travel alone. Women were never left in social situations with men outside their families and were assigned a chaperone to look after them. Commonly, the chaperone was female and might be the girl's mother or an aunt (or sometimes an older, married sister) whose job it was to make sure that nothing inappropriate took place. A servant (like a maid) was not considered an acceptable chaperone as they might be susceptible to being bribed, but a trusted family retainer like a governess

'Marriage is indeed a manoeuvring business.'

Mary Crawford,
Mansfield Park

might fill the role at a pinch. There were strict codes set out for social interaction, which to the modern ear sound excessively formal; it was common to bow or curtsey when you met, for instance, and many women became engaged to men without having ever used their first names or been in a room alone with them. Etiquette also covered how to dress for different occasions. Interestingly, women often wore low-cut outfits (particularly in the evening) and having your cleavage on show was not considered as inappropriate as the more shocking practice of flashing an ankle.

· • • ·

Getting married

LADY DENHAM: How many brothers and sisters have you?

CHARLOTTE: Eleven, ma'am.

LADY DENHAM: Eleven! You will need to marry well! And no doubt they've sent you to Sanditon to find yourself a fortune!

CHARLOTTE: Not at all, ma'am.

LADY DENHAM: Nonsense, of course they have! No shame in that. *Episode 1*

Coming out was building to the main event in a young woman's life – her marriage. When Charlotte Heywood claims she isn't looking for a husband in *Sanditon*, this is so unusual that Lady Denham refuses to believe her. Marriage, although it came with great social advantages, was nevertheless a serious undertaking. Firstly, marriage was for life – divorce was almost unheard of and required the permission of Parliament. The only possible grounds for divorce was the infidelity of the wife and an action could only be pursued by the husband, who retained custody of the children in all cases. It was entirely acceptable for men to be unfaithful and women could not seek a divorce on those or any other grounds. This meant that, once married, a woman had no way out of the arrangement. She also lost many of her legal rights. A married couple was viewed as one entity in law and that entity was the husband. Married women could not own property – everything a woman possessed belonged to her husband and the man had absolute authority over his wife. There was no concept of sexual consent within marriage or possible charge of rape. A man had the right to discipline his wife and that could include locking her up or beating her. This explains, firstly, why men of honour stood up so strongly for women they cared about – women were exceptionally vulnerable. Darcy in *Pride and Prejudice* protects his sister to the point of risking his own life. Secondly, this explains why marriage was taken so seriously – it required a great deal of trust, and sadly that trust was not always merited.

'An engaged woman is always more agreeable than a disengaged. She is satisfied with herself. Her cares are over and she feels that she may exert all her powers of pleasing without suspicion. All is safe with a lady engaged; no harm can be done.'

Henry Crawford,
Mansfield Park

'A woman is not to marry a man merely because she is asked, or because he is attached to her, and can write a tolerable letter.'

Emma Woodhouse, *Emma*

A GEORGIAN CAUTIONARY TALE

The story of Rachel Chiesley, Lady Grange (1679–1745) is a good example of a (presumably happy, if spirited) marriage that went wrong. Rachel started an affair with James Erskine, Lord Grange, in about 1708. He initially refused to marry her when she became pregnant. Rachel, however, threatened him with a pistol and he changed his mind. According to her, they then lived together for nearly twenty-five years 'in great love and peace' and had nine children – four sons and five daughters. When Lady Grange discovered that her husband had a mistress, she followed him, abused him verbally in public, swore at his relations, drank excessively and allegedly threatened to reveal that he was a Jacobite (a serious political offence). Whatever her actions, she was certainly scandalously treated by her husband in return. Trying to pacify her, Erskine offered her a job managing his estate in Scotland while he stayed in London, but the arrangement did not last for long. In 1732, intending to confront her husband, about whom she had heard a troubling rumour, Lady Grange booked a seat on the London coach; but, before she could leave, a party of Highlanders kidnapped her, apparently on Lord Grange's orders. She was taken to the Monach islands and from there to the remotest island in the British Isles, St Kilda, where she was imprisoned for four years. In 1738 she smuggled out a letter describing 'the misserie and sorrow and hunger and hardships of all kindes that I have suffrd', and an expedition was mounted by her sons to rescue her, but she had been moved before it arrived. She died in 1745, still a prisoner. Her grave is in the churchyard at Trumpan on the Isle of Skye.

Below: A portrait of Rachel Chiesley, Lady Grange (1710).

Given this kind of salutary tale, it's not surprising that the decision of who to marry was taken extremely seriously by families who had to balance the possible social advantages of the match with the nature of the man to whom they were effectively handing over their daughter's welfare. This also explains why Sidney Parker is right to be protective of his ward, Georgiana, in *Sanditon*. As an heiress, Georgiana would be extremely vulnerable. If a young woman owned any property (which she might, like Georgiana, have inherited), it was customary to 'entail' that property before the marriage, which meant that her husband could not sell it. The property still became his, though if he died, it might be agreed that it would revert to the woman. As part of this kind of agreement it was common to lay out what income a wife became entitled to on marriage – the allowance that her husband would give her to buy clothes or pay her personal servants, for example. The inheritance that would come to any children of the marriage on the death of the parents was also often specified before the ceremony took place. This was, at least, some kind of safety net, but did not protect women from husbands determined to bully, beat or force them to have sex against their will. It also makes sense of arrangements made between distant relations that kept family money inside the family and meant that women were marrying men their close relatives knew to be fair-minded. If a husband broke an entail, a woman would find it difficult to pursue compensation on her own, and the case would need to be taken up by her male relations.

'The most incomprehensible thing in the world to a man is a woman who rejects his offer of marriage!'

Emma Woodhouse,
Emma

· • • • ·

The dangers of married life

Loss of personal autonomy was not the only danger married women faced, however. Pregnancy and childbirth were hugely hazardous occupations and, with no reliable method of contraception available, in marriage they were all but unavoidable. There was no test for pregnancy – women simply noted that their periods disappeared. When Jane Austen herself was born, she was a month later than her mother expected. With no medical confirmation possible, it must have been easy to miscalculate delivery dates or even undergo an early miscarriage and then conceive straight afterwards. Little was known about obstetrics or gynaecology in the era, and, when a pregnant woman's waters broke and she went into labour, no painkillers or anaesthetics were available. Earlier in the Georgian era, forceps had come into use, the practice regulated by the work of an early 'man-midwife' (or obstetrician), William Smellie (1697–1763). Though many women were initially sceptical of this advance, it helped speed the delivery of some babies. By the Regency, the practice of giving birth in a 'birthing chair' was waning and many women were choosing to have their babies at home in bed. Female midwives were popular, male obstetricians were new to the game, and practices were becoming professionalised. The death rate for mothers was about one per 1,000, which, given average birth rates, trans-

'I shall be very well off, with all the children of a sister I love so much to care about. There will be enough of them, in all probability, to supply every sort of sensation that declining life can need.'

Emma Woodhouse,
Emma

lated to a two to three per cent chance of death during the birth or shortly afterwards.

Despite these risks, with little control over conception, married women often had large families – one study undertaken of aristocratic women between 1760 and 1860 found they had an average of 7.5 children each (this was higher than the overall national average of five children per mother, which may be accounted for by the fact that aristocratic women did not usually breastfeed their children and employed wet-nurses, thus becoming fertile more quickly after giving birth than women lower down the social scale).

Given all the dangers, it's surprising that women got married at all. But the social pressure to do so was huge, and married women enjoyed the social advantages of having more freedom, running their own house and being accorded a far higher level of prestige within the community. Still, some either chose to be or ended up as spinsters – like Jane and her sister, Cassandra. Georgian broadsheets often featured cruel cartoons about dried-up old women, who were dependent on income from jobs like being a governess, or were simply pushed around various family homes, looking after young children or elderly relations.

This doesn't strike a chord with Jane Austen's experience of being unmarried. Her family valued her, although after her father's death it took some time before the Austen women managed to secure a permanent home. Jane and Cassandra Austen remained single for several reasons. Neither of them had a dowry so they had nothing to bring to a marriage but themselves. This was not an attractive proposition and put them at a disadvantage in the marriage market. Both women did, however, receive at least one proposal of marriage each. In Jane's case she decided not to accept Harris Bigg-Wither

Single women have a dreadful propensity for being poor, which is one very strong argument in favour of matrimony.'

Jane Austen to her niece Fanny Knight, 13 March 1817

(see page 15); in Cassandra's, her fiancé Thomas Fowle died in 1797 in the West Indies, on a trip there as chaplain to his cousin Lord Craven's regiment. Military deaths were relatively common: the Napoleonic War wiped out about one in twelve men between 1804 and 1815 – leading to a fact Jane noted in a letter to Cassandra: 'There is a great scarcity of Men in general, & a still greater scarcity of any that were good for much.' Still, if an unmarried woman had money, she had a great deal more control over her life than her married sisters and, despite the social disadvantages, it's easy to understand why some women might have chosen not to undertake the precarious business of matrimony – as Charlotte claims she wants in *Sanditon*.

LADY DENHAM
Anne Reid

—◆—

LADY DENHAM:

What we need at Sanditon is an heiress! If we could get a young heiress
sent here for her health! – and if she was ordered to drink ass's milk, I
could supply her – and then, when she got well, have her fall in love with
Sir Edward! But these young heiresses are in very short supply, I find.
And then there's his sister, Miss Esther, she must marry somebody of
fortune too! It's no use them looking to me for money – my money is all
tied up in great projects, as they well know!

– Episode 1

—◆—

*'But she is very, very mean. I can see no good in her . . .
Thus it is, when rich people are sordid.'*
CHARLOTTE HEYWOOD, *SANDITON*

Lady Denham, played by Anne Reid

The *grande dame* of Sanditon Lady Denham is wealthy, snobby and bossy. Married twice, she has acquired a huge fortune and title and enjoys playing with the hopes of those dependent upon her. Lady Denham is staggeringly forthright and highly suspicious of the motives of everyone around her – both her heirs and incomers like Charlotte Heywood. She is a stakeholder in Sanditon and loves holding her investment over Tom Parker, frequently threatening to withdraw it. This is an old woman who has, in her own eyes, made it and has nothing to lose.

What is the most fun about playing Lady Denham?

She behaves so badly! She's mean and bossy, especially to Kris Marshall, who plays Tom Parker – he takes it very well he's such a good actor. I love that she's so ruthless and domineering and behaves outrageously.

Widows were the women who could be most free in Regency life. Do you think Lady Denham is happy?

She must have lonely moments, though she distracts herself, which is why she takes in Clara and invests so much time in Sanditon. As you get older you need creative projects to keep you busy.

Some of your outfits are really complicated. Which are your favourites?

I loved the brown hat with the feathers that I wear in the first scene. I put it on and I fell in love. I want to wear it around London.

Is playing comedy more difficult than playing drama?

Absolutely. It's an instinct and you either have it or you don't. Alexandra Roach, who plays Diana, has it. She's effortless. And with comedy you know immediately if you've done a good job. I mean, people either laugh or they don't.

Your character has the biggest house in Sanditon but if you were moving there where would you choose to live?

A nice little cottage by the harbour near the beach. And I'd want a boat to potter about in too.

What do you think Lady Denham is afraid of?

She'd hate to be poor. If she lost her money, she'd jump off the pier (not that Sanditon has a pier.) Yes, I think if she lost everything, that would be the worst for her. That and growing old.

· • • • ·

Georgian beauty

MAKE-UP

In the Regency era, the fashion was for a 'natural' look. Earlier generations had worn heavy make-up but, as an 1811 fashion guide recommends, Regency women preferred to go along with 'the general principles of nature'. This did not mean that make-up was not used, but women stopped painting cupid's bow lips and flirtatious fake moles as they had in the late eighteenth century and focused on making themselves look healthy. This was ironic as some of the make-up available was toxic. The white pigment used to colour face foundation was lead-based, and commonly rouge might be made of tin – another poison. Long-term use of these cosmetics made many women ill – lead face paint in particular caused severe abdominal pain, among other side effects. While women made their own preparations, there was also huge growth in the availability of commercially produced items. Among the non-toxic make-up on offer, some was excellent, and the brand Pears (still known today for its soaps) produced White Imperial Powder, which was like modern-day highlighter, and Pears Liquid Blooms of Roses – a rouge – which came in several shades. Some women took exception to wearing any make-up, however, perhaps because heavy make-up was commonly associated with the

stage and therefore also with prostitutes. For these ladies, pinching their cheeks and biting their lips would have been the best they could do.

PERFUME

Given the strong smells of city life and the fact that people bathed far less often than they do in the present day (though washing daily using water in a bowl was common), most people who could afford it wore perfume. Scents were made, as today, from oils that could be mixed with alcohol or sold as 'waters' usually distilled from flowers. The most popular scents were generally floral – lavender, lily, jasmine and rose. Some perfume oils were hugely expensive to make and therefore highly prized – like the smell of violets. Some people favoured spicier concoctions that included musky scents like cinnamon, nutmeg, clove and sandalwood, which would have been imported alongside citrus oils such as orange and lemon. At the top end, perfumes were mixed with ambergris, the fatty secretion of the sperm whale, to make them last longer on the skin. The whaling industry was widespread for both meat and whale oil, and ambergris was widely available (if costly). Apothecaries often made perfumes for their clients as well as medicines and they guarded their recipes carefully.

HAIR

In 1795 the prime minister, William Pitt the Younger, imposed a tax on hair powder, which failed to raise the revenue he had hoped for because people abandoned the wearing of powdered wigs. Pitt's tax raised just 46,000 guineas and people turned to pomades to scent and mould their hair. These were made from animal and vegetable waxes (i.e. fats) scented with oils.

In the Regency era, the fashion for women was classical with the hair drawn back from the face and ringlets hanging to the side or the back. In 1810 Lady Caroline Lamb (for a short time Lord Byron's mistress) scandalised society by cutting her hair short, but society quickly became accustomed to Caroline's style and for a while it became fashionable for a lady to wear shorter hair with ribbons.

For men, the fashion was to be clean-shaven and have short hair – inspired, like so many Regency looks, by Greek and Roman statues. This became known as the 'Bedford crop'

Lady Caroline Lamb.

after Lord Bedford adopted it in protest at Pitt's tax. Also popular for gentlemen were the Caesar, Titus and Brutus hairstyles, all named after statues of these famous Roman figures.

BEHIND THE SCENES

Hair and make-up

The hair and make-up trailer on the *Sanditon* set has its own dog – Barney – a bichon frise and poodle cross who belongs to Helen Tucker, the hair and make-up designer. 'Barney calms down everyone who comes in,' Helen says. 'He's therapy.'

The trailer has six chairs and is used for all the main cast members, with a larger, separate room that is kept aside for crowd scenes. On shooting days on location, the make-up team travels to the site on a customised truck. The team consists of six make-up artists and two trainees, with extra make-up artists brought in to help on busy days. 'The brief for this production is to make it look young and poppy,' Helen explains. 'The make-up is minimal and free-spirited. If a cast member gets hot or sweaty we don't dampen down the look – it's far sexier to have loose hair and a little bit of shine now and then. I want them to look dewy. The most difficult thing has been to work with the lighting. For the indoor scenes the lighting has mostly been moody and I need to put on more make-up to make the cast look really good.'

Helen works closely with the actors, often buying in products that they already use and are comfortable with. 'I've heard horror stories about black actors arriving on other sets and there not being appropriate products for

their skin, so I wanted to make sure that everyone was catered for. Crystal [playing Georgiana Lambe] recommended a great range by Rihanna, which we used. We also kept her hair natural – I think she really liked that.'

For the hair design the team decided to use as few wigs as possible – mostly for the actors playing servants. The trailer houses an oven to bake the styles into place. A series of 'flunky' wigs was created. 'It was quite unusual – normally we'd go for contrast but we did the exact opposite. We had flunkies wearing sand-coloured wigs on the beach and black wigs in Lady Denham's house, which is all black marble. The Parkers' staff had a kind of donkey colour. I wanted to distinguish the footmen – almost like teams.' Lady Denham, played by Anne Reid, is the only main character who wears a wig. 'We used the wig to add height,' Helen explains. 'But even then, I wanted to keep the set quite loose so it wasn't too perfect.' With the rest of the principal cast Helen and her team used lots of ribbons to add movement to the hair design.

Their work on set was backed up by local businesses, who cut and coloured some of the principal characters' real hair.

The make-up truck is also used to produce the prosthetics for special effects. 'We have five different recipes for blood,' Helen explains. 'It's all fake, of course – we have fresh, congealed, old and runny blood, all made here. We add washing-up liquid to emulsify it and burnt sugar to add texture. Prosthetic wounds need lots of touch-ups while shooting so they stay looking fresh. It's long hours and it's a busy department, but none of us would want to do anything else.'

The language of the fan

LADY DENHAM: Clara, my parasol.

CLARA: Yes, aunt. Of course. Here it is.

LADY DENHAM: My fan.

Clara gives her the fan.
Lady Denham makes a big show of using it.

LADY DENHAM (pointedly to ESTHER):
At least someone considers my
welfare.   *Episode 5*

*'Men have the sword,
women have the fan and
the fan is probably as
effective a weapon!'*

Joseph Addison

Fans were a vital fashion accessory for the well-dressed
Georgian lady. In the Regency era, the vogue was for relatively plain fans to match the white muslin dresses favoured
by those in the know. Fans were expensive luxury items,
often imported from specialist makers in France, Italy
and China. The sticks or ribs could be made from wood,
mother-of-pearl or ivory, and the leaf hand-painted on
silk, satin or gauze and decorated with gems. Cheaper fans
made from printed paper were also widely available and
often depicted current news stories or famous paintings.

*Opposite: A fan from
the Regency era.*

An upper-class English woman would own different fans to match different outfits and it was considered an art to use a fan so as to showcase elegant wrists and hands. Fans were also a means to flirt and send signals to eligible young men.

A fan folded against a lady's chin announced her interest, while a fan snapped closed was definitely a rejection. This meant lovers could secretly communicate their intentions in public places like dances or even just at dinner.

CLARA BRERETON
Lily Sacofsky

LADY DENHAM:
Clara ... plays very tolerably. Well, sit down girl and display your talent!

– Episode 1

ESTHER:
What did happen with Clara Brereton, Edward? Something has clearly gone wrong.

– Episode 2

ESTHER:
We have to dislodge that little interloper, Clara Brereton. She will insist on getting in the way.

– Episode 2

Clara Brereton, played by Lily Sacofsky

Clara is one of Lady Denham's poor relations. She lives with Lady Denham and hopes that she might inherit the old lady's fortune. Sweet and subservient, her background is shrouded in mystery, but she is determined not to return to where she came from to the point of self-harm, and there is nothing she will not do to retain her position at Denham Place. This puts her into a head-to-head battle with the Denham siblings, which is complicated by the fact that Edward finds himself genuinely attracted to her.

What was your most difficult scene to play?
Definitely the scene where we were bathing in the sea – it was absolutely freezing!

What was your first Jane Austen experience?
This is my first Jane Austen experience.

Sex is absolutely taboo for an unmarried Regency lady, but Clara has a lot of experience. Did that feel dangerous?
It felt very dangerous. This was not a sexually liberated time for women; it was commonly believed that women did not

derive pleasure from sex. The stakes are extremely high, and reputation is everything in this world. There is no contraception and no protection from disease, so sex for a woman is a great risk. If Lady Denham found out what Clara had been up to, she would lose everything. However, for Clara, sex is currency . . . and it's the only currency she has.

How important is authenticity to you in terms of the period? How does playing a period part vary from other contemporary roles?

I like to know as much as I possibly can about a period before beginning a role. The time in which your character lived and the experiences they have had is important in shaping who they are. Learning about the life Clara had before moving to Sanditon was important to my work so that I knew just how different it was to the beauty and grandeur of Sanditon House. It varies from modern roles because the imaginative world is so different. You have to create in your mind a time that is alien to you and figure out how you can relate to it.

Were the costumes and make-up/hair difficult to wear?

The corsets were sometimes challenging after a long day and it takes a bit longer to go to the loo! I wouldn't have been without them, though; they make you feel trapped . . . which is the right feeling.

What advice would you give to Clara?

I don't really have any advice for Clara because I think she is how she is out of necessity. She is a victim of circumstance. She must survive. I wish I could change things for her and give her some security.

· · • • • ·

The main event: the ball

TOM PARKER: Lady Denham, ladies and gentlemen, let me welcome you to our first ball of the season. Our committee has agreed that there will be no standing on ceremony here – if a lady wishes to be introduced to a gentleman, or vice versa, I will be happy to do the honours. Let good fellowship prevail – and I hope you have all come prepared to dance.   *Episode 1*

TOM PARKER: How happy I am to see the light return to your eyes, Charlotte.

CHARLOTTE: There is nothing like dancing to restore one's spirits!   *Episode 6*

Jane Austen's novels place great emphasis on ball scenes and Jane herself loved dancing. For single people during the Regency, a ball provided one of the few opportunities for them to meet prospective partners from a wider pool than

simply their family and friends. Up until around 1810 the main dances were country dances like the cotillion (danced in sets of four couples) and the Scotch reel, which was danced between sets of more than that. After the Napoleonic Wars, the quadrille (danced usually with five people) and the waltz (scandalisingly intimate as couples had to embrace and simply dance with each other) were introduced to the English ballroom. Etiquette around dancing meant that it was frowned upon to dance with the same partner more than twice and, if you turned down a request to dance, you would have to sit out for the rest of the party. This meant people tended to join in and that guests could not be 'hogged' by one partner. A man could only ask a woman to dance if he had been introduced to her (though this could usually be arranged, one way or another).

Balls were about much more than dancing. Running from around 8 p.m. until at least the early hours of the morning, if not until dawn, they took a huge amount of planning and investment. Public balls took place at the assembly rooms and were funded by the sale of tickets, but upper-class hostesses prided themselves on throwing private balls, by invitation, at their own residences (both in town and in the country). Often the date of an event was chosen to coincide with the full moon so that the roads would be well lit for guests arriving or leaving. Armies of servants were employed to clean and ready the rooms and serve the guests. Decorations were put up – flowers and garlands were common, and the dance floor would be embellished with chalk images. This served two purposes: one, simply to look nice and, two, to stop guests slipping as they danced. Wax candles were expensive – a luxury ordinary families certainly couldn't afford – and keeping a ball well illuminated

would require hundreds of them. Ballrooms were often decorated with mirrors and hung with crystal chandeliers, which helped amplify the light. Musicians were engaged and in some areas there was great competition between hostesses to secure the most talented groups for their event. As well as dancing, side rooms were usually set up for card games. A bar would feature and food was served between 11 p.m. and just after midnight. This could be anything from hot port, soup, pies, cakes and sweetmeats to a proper sit-down meal.

A good ball could make a hostess's name and, if you were single, change your life, introducing you to a prospective partner and giving you the freedom to flirt, experiment, talk without other people overhearing and even touch each other. This happens in several Jane Austen novels – *Pride and Prejudice* and *Emma,* for example. Each of the balls in *Sanditon* marks a key stage in Charlotte's relationship with Sidney Parker, as they move from distrusting each other to finding each other increasingly attractive. For Georgian women brought up with restrictive rules and ever-present chaperones, no wonder it was exhilarating.

*The drawing room in
St James's Palace, London, 1809.*

BEHIND THE SCENES

Going to the ball

As in a real Regency season, the series features more than one ball over its eight episodes and this was a challenge for the production team. 'A ball has to have a wow factor. These are fairy-tale moments,' enthuses Grant Montgomery, the production designer. All the ball scenes were shot on the set for Lady Denham's house, which had to be re-dressed for each one.

The first ball was themed using light colours. 'I wanted it to look like a Zeffirelli production,' Montgomery explains. 'We put in a lot of mirrors and used white and gold everywhere, like the Palace of Versailles. All the balls were lit using real candles and the team had two different sets of gold candles made for the first ball, some with double wicks so they burned more brightly but also more quickly.' The first ball was shot from Charlotte's point of view as much as possible to take the viewer on the journey with her into Sanditon society.

The second ball had a silver and white. 'It had to be more like an installation – a themed party. A lot of the scenes feature fog outside so this was to be like the fog clearing and suddenly you were in the Forest of Arden,' he explains. 'The Regency super-rich knew no bounds. They were very cosmopolitan and I had this idea to bring blossom trees indoors and create a magical world.

Music

Writing and curating the music for the series, composer Ruth Barrett wanted to bring the Regency to life, not only with the more traditional sound palette of genteel waltzes associated with Jane Austen, but with folk music from all over the British Isles that would have been sung and played by the whole spectrum of society. She scouted the Celtic Connections festival in Glasgow with singer Gillie Mackenzie, with whom she had previously worked, to find musicians who could create the right sound. 'I wanted to use music that was intoxicating,' she says. 'We started the Sanditon ball with a waltz, but then I chose tracks that sped up in tempo to create what would have been the real, wild party music of Georgian Britain, with fiddles, whistles, guitar and drum. Then, for the ball in London, I adapted some Renaissance music with Celtic harp and baroque viola.' But music was not only the preserve of the upper classes; it was important in day-to-day life too. 'There was no radio or iPods, so people just sang as they worked,' Ruth explains. Barrett also included *puirt à beul*, a Gaelic singing technique from both Scotland and Ireland, in the score, performed by Gaelic singer Julie Fowlis. 'This is where we come from, musically — it's as much part of our musical heritage as nursery rhymes and the work of classical composers,' Barrett says.

'For the balls, we wanted to use folk music — it was very popular at the time. It's something different from the usual Jane Austen soundtrack.'

Ruth Barrett, composer

In addition, Barrett wrote original music for the series' score, creating the title track as well as main themes for each of the characters. 'I want to give the soundscape a gritty feel – something that will get people in the gut. That hasn't been done before with Austen but it's absolutely authentic to the time.'

SANDITON PLAYLIST

Sanditon Theme
'Glory in the Meeting House'
'*Tha Fionnlagh Ag Innearach*'
'Black is the Colour'
Chaconne from Purcell's *Fairy-Queen*

The racy Georgians

While middle- and upper-class women lived protected lives, the world around them was more venal. Prostitution was widespread and references to it appear in many cartoons and news-sheets of the period. Some historians estimate that as many as twenty per cent of young women in London in the late eighteenth century were involved in the sex trade. Guidebooks to Regency 'nightlife' included reviews and costs for different brothels and recommendations for individual women on the game. Prices varied hugely depending on the woman's situation, her beauty and her skill set. Most prostitutes were working class, but if they could manage to appear like a young, well-educated lady they could command high fees; and a clever upper-class courtesan who played the game well could expect to make a fortune on which she could retire. The long-

CATCHING an ELEPHANT.

MAGDALEN CHAPEL.
London Pub. 1st Feby 1800 at R.Ackermann's Repository of Arts 101 Strand.

Left: Two prostitutes encourage a man into the Royal Bagnio in Bagnio Court. Bagnios were resorts or spas, some of which had a reputation for seedy goings-on.

Above: Magdalen Hospital in London, a charitable organisation for 'fallen' women.

term mistress of the Prince of Wales, for example, was promised £20,000 (though this sum was not actually paid to her). The reality was that prostitutes who could find a man to set them up in residence somewhere often became well-kept mistresses. The most famous example of this was Harriette Wilson, a courtesan who wrote a memoir in 1825 about becoming the mistress of William, Lord Craven, at the age of fifteen, which effectively set her up for life.

Georgians had mixed feelings about the trade in sex.

People were fairly religious and disapproved of what they saw (or tried to ignore) around them – especially when it came to their own sisters and daughters. In the late eighteenth century several houses of correction (often known as Magdelene Houses) were set up across the country to reform 'prostitutes'. This term was loose and reformers and legal documents of the day used it for any woman who had sex outside of marriage (including those who were not married but lived with a partner). Women could be incarcerated without trial in the Magdelene House, where they would be trained in a trade (often becoming laundry women). In some cases families admitted their own daughters to these institutions – perhaps because they felt the girls were out of their control.

Although the term 'prostitute' was a loose one, being paid for sex was rife and the reality was that large sections of society were fairly forgiving towards women who had sold themselves going on to marry respectably where they could. Certainly for some women prostitution was an interlude in which they engaged to get over a difficult financial time in their lives. Prostitution did not carry a jail sentence until 1820.

With medical knowledge low, venereal disease was rife. Generally known as the 'pox', syphilis was widespread and incurable. Customers might also contract the 'clap', or gonorrhoea. Rates of infection were high: one modern study using Georgian hospital records for the town of Chester discovered that over eight per cent of the population of both sexes had contracted syphilis by the age of thirty-five within the city limits. In the same county, the figures for the countryside suggest that people were more abstemious, with less than one per cent of the population infected. Both rates

'The Regency is rambunctious, and the hotel in Sanditon had to reflect that. Many men in the period had just come back from war. They could handle themselves physically. This isn't a world that Austen writes about directly but we hear about the "regiment" in Pride and Prejudice, *for example. I wanted to show the gambling that went on, the games of billiards, the prostitutes. The things that were hidden from Austen. Sanditon, after all, was a frontier town.'*

Grant Montgomery, production designer

are far higher than those for sexually transmitted diseases today. Lack of medical knowledge did not stop Georgian doctors trying to cure their patients of these diseases; they employed purgatives and poisons, including injections of mercury into the penis, and mercury pills commonly prescribed for syphilis. These caused loosening (and loss) of the teeth, ulcers and neurological damage.

Contraception was unreliable. Condoms were available – made from animal gut or oiled cloth. Most prostitutes relied on customers pulling out, which was ineffective. Illegal terminations among prostitutes were common and some 'farmed out' their babies, sending them into the care of poor families, so they could continue to make money plying their trade.

· • • ·

Princess Caraboo:
a Regency hoax

A couple of years before Charlotte Heywood helps the Parkers recover from their carriage accident in Sanditon, in real-life Regency England a scam was afoot. In April 1817 a cobbler in Almondsbury, Gloucestershire, came across a disorientated young woman wearing exotic clothes. She apparently spoke no English and the cobbler took her to the local magistrate, Samuel Worrall. After examining the woman, who seemed to call herself Caraboo and insisted on sleeping on the floor, the magistrate declared she was a beggar and sent her to Bristol to be tried for vagrancy.

While Caraboo was in prison, a Portuguese sailor who was also incarcerated there claimed that he spoke Caraboo's language and identified her as a princess from the island of Javasu in the Indian Ocean. He said she had been kidnapped by pirates and had jumped ship into the Bristol Channel from where she had swum to shore.

Horrified that he had sent an exotic, foreign princess to jail, Samuel Worrall and his American-born wife, Elizabeth, insisted on offering the princess hospitality. For ten weeks they hosted her, introducing her to local Gloucestershire society. Caraboo could fence and use a bow and arrow. She apparently prayed to Allah-Talla – one of the formal names for God in Islam. She also swam naked. On examination it was found she had strange marks on the back of her head, which were thought to be of ritual *significance*.

Princess Caraboo became a celebrity. National newspapers picked up her story and ran pictures of her dressed in exotic robes. Eventually, a boarding-house keeper from Bristol contacted the Worralls. She recognised Caraboo, who was, she said, a cobbler's daughter from Devon called Mary Willcocks. The marks on Caraboo's head were scars from the medical procedure of 'cupping', which she had undergone as a child. No doubt embarrassed, the Worralls arranged to send Caraboo to Philadelphia in America at their expense in June 1817. Interest in Caraboo was high and, in the September of the same year, a letter in the *Bristol Journal* purporting to be from Sir Hudson Lowe, Napoleon's jailer on St Helena, said that Caraboo had escaped the ship taking her to America and that Napoleon himself had fallen in love with her and wanted to marry her. There is absolutely no evidence to verify Lowe's story.

The next time we hear of Caraboo she is in America, appearing on stage. By the end of 1817, she wrote to the Worralls from New York complaining that she had become too famous. In 1824 she returned to England, where she unsuccessfully put herself 'on show'. Four years later she married, had a daughter and settled down – in 1839 she was running a business, selling leeches to doctors at the Bristol Infirmary Hospital. Caraboo died in 1864, ending the tale of a famous Regency hoax that had played into so many stories beloved of Regency society – exotic tales of derring-do and adventure – an ordinary woman who became an international showgirl.

Princess Caraboo, alias for Mary Willcocks.

· • • ·

Wards

CROWE: But if a fellow might ask without getting his head bit off - what is your history with her.

SIDNEY PARKER: I am simply handling her affairs until she comes of age. Not a job I wanted, and I'm finding it damn irksome. The girl misses the homeland, hates the climate here and doesn't care for being treated as a curiosity.

BABINGTON: And she doesn't care for you

SIDNEY PARKER: Pretty much takes exception to everything I say or do. *Episode 1*

A ward is a young person who is in the care (or guardianship) of an adult. In *Sanditon*, Georgiana Lambe is Sidney Parker's ward, a responsibility he is not pleased about. However, it wasn't unusual in an era of high mortality rates for parents to nominate who would care for their children in the event of their deaths. The term 'wardship' was in use in England from medieval times. Originally, it only applied

Right: Edward Austen Knight.

to wealthy families and was less a way to care for orphaned children than a means of administering their estates. When valuable lands were inherited by a child, the income from their property (and the right to profit from their marriage) went to the person who owned their wardship. Girls were wards until the age of sixteen and boys until twenty-one, and the rights to the money generated by their estates and marriages could be bought and sold.

By Georgian times, this practice had softened, and there was more emphasis on caring for orphaned children and organising their education and domestic arrangements, but guardianship still had an element of looking after the child's inheritance and negotiating any dowry or marriage. In the Regency period, guardianship usually continued for children of either sex until they were twenty-one and the children in question did not need to be orphaned. There were a number of ways this might work. Jane Austen's brother Edward, for example, wasn't brought up with his siblings at Steventon, but was fostered by wealthy cousins who were childless – the Knights. This meant he effectively became their son, including taking their surname and, eventually, inheriting the Knight fortune. It acted as a way of keeping family money inside the family.

Poor children who were orphaned were taken in by neighbours or relations, or became 'wards of the parish', which meant the local church might buy apprenticeships for them or farm them out to orphanages – as in *Oliver Twist*.

With no legal mechanism for adoption in Britain until the 1920s, these kinds of guardianships provided a safety net for children and young people, albeit largely unregulated. The truth is, the practice wasn't without its risks and there was nobody tasked with ensuring that guardians behaved in

'To be gawped at and served up for the general amusement. To be sneered at and laughed at. A public spectacle. Here we have the pineapple and here we have the Negress. Feast your eyes!'

Georgiana Lambe, *Sanditon*

the best interests of their ward. Georgiana Lambe's fortune of £100,000 makes her an exceptionally wealthy young lady, but Sidney's frustration at having dominion over her and the move to England, with all its unfamiliar etiquette, puts her in a difficult position. It's no wonder she feels she doesn't belong and has no control over her life. And for Sidney the situation is also trying. Responsibility for a widespread range of family members and associates often fell to men of fortune in this era, who were expected to help out poorer relations and could be appointed by friends as custodians of their children in their will. There was no way to turn down this duty in law. In *Sanditon*, Sidney talks about taking on his responsibilities; however, the reality is that he doesn't know how to handle headstrong Georgiana, and he is only willing to do the bare minimum, settling her in Mrs Griffiths' care away from the temptations of London.

Mr Gladstone's Orphanage, Hawarden.

· • • ·

Vulnerability

Women were vulnerable in so many ways in Georgian society – physically as well as legally. However, the reality was that kidnappings and elopements were, sadly, not unheard of. Over the course of the eighteenth century law makers tried to legislate against women being kidnapped and forced into relationships. In fact, the Marriage Act of 1753 invalidated marriages if either the bride or groom were under twenty-one and did not have the permission of their parents or guardians. It also stated that a marriage had to be announced in church three weeks before the ceremony, which had to take place in public. A special licence could be obtained to circumvent this, but it cost £5 (a huge sum of money for most people).

Parliament's intention in passing this legislation was to stop illicit marriages, particularly if they took advantage of innocent women and addressed something that had been a problem for a long time. The practice known as 'irregular marriage' was usually performed outside church, privately, by unscrupulous (or sympathetic, depending on whose side you were on) Anglican ministers. However, the new law only applied in England and what actually happened when it came into force, was that young lovers, as well as more sinister, forced marriages, were displaced north to Scotland, where the law was different.

'I have just had a letter from Jane, with such dreadful news. It cannot be concealed from any one. My youngest sister has left all her friends – has eloped; – has thrown herself into the power of – of Mr Wickham. They are gone off together from Brighton. You know him too well to doubt the rest. She has no money, no connections, nothing that can tempt him to – she is lost for ever.'

Elizabeth Bennet,
Pride and Prejudice

This trip was a big undertaking. The border was at least a four-day carriage ride from London along the Great North Road. The most famous town to elope to was Gretna Green, but there was a brisk trade in weddings in most border towns, including Coldstream and Lamberton, where, under Scottish law, marriage from twelve years of age for girls and fourteen years of age for boys was legal without parental consent.

The status of women and the emphasis put on both their virginity and virtue meant that if a woman was kidnapped, unless she managed to get away quickly, she often felt she had no choice but to go through with the wedding, as her good name would be ruined simply for being abducted. Added to this, the legal position of women as a possession of their male relations meant that, once married, a woman's family could do little to protect or reclaim the abducted woman. Where the abduction was agreed between young lovers, this was less of an issue. But there are several cases of women being taken against their will. In 1826 the Shrigley Abduction scandalised Georgian society when a

Ellen Turner.

fifteen-year-old heiress, Ellen Turner, was taken to Gretna Green against her will by Edward Gibbon Wakefield. Uncommonly (and only because of the huge sums of money involved) the marriage was overturned by the Parliament at Westminster, and Gibbon Wakefield and his brother (who had helped him) were sent to prison for three years. This was highly unusual and most kidnapped women had to try to make marriage work with their kidnappers.

The obvious injustice and drama of this make abduction and elopement key story devices in Regency novels, where there are significantly more happy endings than the practice incurred in real life.

5
BRITISH LIFE
in the
REGENCY

· • • • ·

WHEN THE PRODUCTION team met to design the overall concept for *Sanditon*, they wanted to create a world a lot wider than that inhabited by a traditional Jane Austen adaptation. A world that reflected all of Regency society, from the bottom to the top, with its divisive politics and its grit and glory. They drew on material from the real history of the times. So, what was Regency Britain actually like?

In 1819, the year the TV production of *Sanditon* is set, Britain was still emerging from its decisive triumph over Napoleon at Waterloo in 1815, hot on the heels of the Peninsular War which had lasted for six years and had been extremely violent, with British troops made up of convicts as well as enlisted soldiers. Wellington himself called these men 'the scum of the earth', but also said that they had made him proud. With Robert Jenkinson, 2nd Earl of Liverpool, as Conservative prime minister, the country was poised for the Industrial Revolution to take off and, with that huge sea change in the economy, there was a tide of radicalism and dissent approaching. Fighting Napoleon had been costly, with war pensions in the aftermath also costing a fortune; the Prince Regent spent money like water and the country's finances were in a parlous state – in fact, income tax was charged for the very first time in order to cover the costs of the Napoleonic Wars. It was instituted as a temporary measure but has never been repealed.

Ordinary people felt under pressure. The Corn Laws of

1815 had been passed to protect the price of British grain, but this meant that food was relatively costly and disaffection was in the air, with a number of political associations campaigning against the government, agitating for change. The very poorest in society were literally starving. In 1817 Lord Liverpool was so disquieted by the mounting anger and the actions of these political groups that he suspended the writ of habeas corpus, which meant that the government could arrest people and imprison them indefinitely without having to take them to trial.

Above: An engraving of Napoleon surrendering to Captain Maitland in 1808.

Part of what was causing the unrest was that the world was changing in two ways. The end of the eighteenth century had seen the Enlightenment – a movement into modern thought in philosophy, religion and economics that questioned the traditional order. Adam Smith had written *The Wealth of Nations* and in a stroke had created the idea of the free market. David Hume had put forward a compelling case for atheism, among other philosophical endeavours. On top of this, ordinary people were becoming more literate and were educating themselves to question the way things were done both politically and economically.

At the turn of the century, Britain was a largely rural economy, but industrial advances meant that work was becoming automated and this was fired by the might of the British Empire, which enabled raw materials to be brought into the country ready for use in factories making manufactured goods that could be sold at a profit. This was a big change in a short period. In 1801 about twenty per cent of the population lived in towns, but by 1851 that had risen to around fifty per cent. The profits were potentially huge for investors but large groups of working-class people were forced off the land and into towns where they were driven into extreme poverty. A group of political campaigners called the Luddites wrecked the new machinery whenever they could. This was a serious offence and if caught the penalty was death by hanging. Some people protested more peacefully. In March 1817 a group called the Blanketeers set out to march from Manchester to London but were stopped at Stockport by troops.

It was not unreasonable of people to try to increase their rights and conditions, but, having seen the French Revolution only a few years before, the British government and ruling classes were determined to come down hard on anything that could be viewed as radical. Elsewhere in the world revolutions were underway. In Argentina in 1817 General José de San Martín was on his way to liberating Chile and Peru, resulting in Chilean independence from Spain – a conflict that continued until 1826 and called into question overseas empires of the very kind that the British economy counted on.

It's hardly surprising then that the same summer we see Sanditon unfolding on our screens, Lord Liverpool sanctioned the Peterloo Massacre in Manchester in August, when cavalry charged a crowd of over 60,000 peaceful demonstrators who were petitioning for reform of parliamentary representation. Fifteen people died and hundreds were wounded. Liverpool's government subsequently passed legislation to prevent people gathering for peaceful demonstrations and also gagged free speech. Ordinary people were outraged. In retaliation, the following year a conspiracy was foiled in its attempt to assassinate Liverpool and some of his cabinet ministers.

Lord Liverpool succeeded in easing the tense situation to some degree. He supported the admission of Catholics to become magistrates, to serve as senior officers in the armed forces and, if they fulfilled specific conditions, to get the vote. As we'll look at later in this chapter, this was an era when slavery was also on its way to abolition – so positive change was around as well as negative. But it wasn't enough to stop the legitimate protests of the many people whose lives were being changed for the worse.

Below: A wood engraving of the Peterloo Massacre, 16 August 1819.

This is all a world away from Sanditon's middle-class seaside idyll, but it is certainly something that the working-class men who were building Tom Parker's dream would have been aware of – as would most of the more upper-class men who would have read news periodicals of the day (these were less likely to have been picked up by women).

The British Empire

This is also an era in which British influence was increasing abroad. Britain had lost its American colonies in the American War of Independence in 1783 (a fact King George III lamented hugely before he went 'mad'). Although the American colonies were among Britain's oldest and most populous, having lost them, Britain turned its attention to the rest of the world.

Initially, the British Empire was not a function of the British government. Various settlements had come under British control, not because of military action, but because British companies had set up trading posts there. By 1817, there were established British trading posts in Canada, Australia, India, Singapore, Penang, Labuan and the West Indies (where Sidney Parker started his business), as well as emerging outposts in Africa – James Island, the Gambia River, the Cape of Good Hope and in South Africa. While the British crown had some oversight, these were self-managing colonies – a result of the fact that the British Empire was not planned, in any respect, but rather grew out of individual companies taking an interest in locations where there was a profit to be made. Up until the early 1800s, the deal had been that the colonies provided raw materials exclusively to Britain and also became the exclusive market for British goods. Though the slave trade itself

'I read Matthew Parker's The Sugar Barons *as initial research for the character. It chronicles early sugar traders in the 1820s in Antigua. The heat, the adventure, the horror. All things Sidney Parker would have encountered on his travels.'*

Theo James, playing
Sidney Parker

(i.e. the shipping of people) had become illegal in 1807, it still fired colonial economies by providing free labour. Over the course of the Napoleonic Wars, Britain had gained further territories – Malta, Saint Lucia, Malacca, British Columbia, Trinidad and Ceylon (now Sri Lanka) were added to the list, as well as additional territories in India. In the century from 1815 onwards, around 10 million square miles were added to British territory and 400 million people became British colonial citizens. Informally (not in government), Britain also exerted control over the economies of China, Argentina and Siam (now Thailand).

This expansion, in addition to the fact that the end of the Napoleonic Wars left Britain as the principal naval and imperial power in what was a relatively peaceful period, opened the door to the growth of Britain's empire. Gradually, the colonies became less the business of individual British companies and more the business of the Foreign Office at Whitehall. For ordinary middle- and upper-class people – most of those featured in *Sanditon* – this meant opportunities for their sons to do business abroad and for the family to benefit from goods that were being imported.

Culturally, this lure represented itself in all sorts of ways: there was a vogue for Chinese and Indian styles in furniture and fashion, which had started with the Prince Regent's exotic designs for Brighton Pavilion. People were fascinated by greenhouses, where specimens brought home from around the world could be propagated. They were also intrigued by unusual new foods – as evidenced by Lady Denham's pineapple luncheon. In 1820 many of the imported objects were in the hands of private owners and collectors, but over the coming years the first public museums and art galleries would begin to display collections of artefacts from around the world. To educate and prepare the people who would be going out to the colonies, John Murray, Jane Austen's publisher, brought out the first travel guides. These were not like travel guides today, which are written to a template that gives a standardised picture of weather, food and places of interest to visit. Murray simply hunted for someone who had been to the place he wanted to create a guide for and asked them to write about their experiences. Some of these early guides include chapters about the author's particular interests (in one, the man – a keen chicken fancier – gives an exhaustive account of the way locals keep their chickens and of the exotic breeds he discovered while he was abroad!). These guidebooks were a huge success and other publishers began to emulate Murray's innovation.

It is hardly a surprise that young men like Sidney Parker and his friends – the cream of British society – felt what we would call today 'over-entitled'. They grew up in an expanding economy that prided itself on dominating the cultures of the places where it traded.

· • • • ·

Cricket

CHARLOTTE: I assume you are here for the cricket, Mr Parker.

SIDNEY: You never seem short of assumptions, Miss Heywood. *Episode 5*

'Cricket is a magical game. I played a lot when I was younger. It's one of those games that if you can survive mentally, you will do well physically.'

**Jack Fox, playing
Sir Edward Denham**

Cricket is generally believed to have first been played in south-east England in the sixteenth century. Games with balls and bats that involved running exist all over the world, but cricket is an English tradition. By the eighteenth century it had become a national sport boasting a long-standing roster of county teams playing against each other, with the results reported in newspapers. A system of patronage emerged, which meant prizes were donated and the organisation of games was funded – or sometimes just hosted – by upmarket enthusiasts like the 2nd Duke of Richmond, who drew up a code of practice for matches to standardise the rules and regulate gambling.

By the end of the eighteenth century, the game had been 'exported' to British colonies, arriving in North America, Australia and the West Indies early on, and New Zealand and South Africa by the time *Sanditon* is set in the early nineteenth century. During the Napoleonic Wars the sport suffered a lull in England because so many men were engaged in fighting. This led to a lack of investment in matches, which were generally underwritten by a wealthy donor. But games were resumed in 1815 after the Battle of Waterloo, and English cricket took up from where it had left off.

In 1817, when Jane Austen wrote the first eleven chapters of *Sanditon*, there was a match-fixing scandal, which culminated in the most celebrated player of the day, William Lambert, being banned from Lord's Cricket Ground in London forever. This is also a period in which the game developed and there were heated debates over which methods of bowling should be allowed.

While the Women's Cricket Association was not founded until 1926, there is a long history of women's matches both across England and the British Empire. Usually, these were played by all-women teams and the action was not always genteel. Some matches pitted teams of single women against teams of married women (ouch) and, in 1747, at a women's game between Charlton and Westdean and Chilgrove, crowd trouble erupted, causing the match to spill over into a second day.

'The greatest cricket match that was played in this part of England was on Friday, the 26th of last month, on Gosden Common, near Guildford, between eleven maids of Bramley and eleven maids of Hambledon, all dressed in white. The Bramley maids had blue ribbons and the Hambledon maids red ribbons on their heads. The Bramley girls got 119 notches and the Hambledon girls 127. The girls bowled, batted, ran and catches as well as most men could do in that game.'

Reading Mercury, 26 July 1745

Cricket match

The inspiration for the cricket match came to Grant Montgomery, the production designer, in a flash. 'I wanted it to look like a Jack Vettriano painting,' he says. 'I could just see it, with big umbrellas on the beach and the scale of the sky. Originally, it was supposed to be in a field, but this was going to look so much better.' The team worked hard on getting the detail right, sourcing and sometimes making props like the Regency cricket bats, which were shorter and thicker than the modern design.

· • • • ·

The regatta

TOM PARKER: The river alive with a flotilla of boats – all shapes and sizes. The banks teeming with spectators – the ladies attired in the finest white dresses, and the gentlemen in straw hats! What do you say to it, Mary? Is it not a brilliant notion? *Episode 3*

Regattas were popular around the coast of England in the early nineteenth century. There was already a long tradition of British boat-building and sailing and it was natural that this would extend to racing. These races could take the form of sailing races at sea or on a river. The word 'regatta' comes from Venetian slang for 'contest' and was probably brought back to England by upper-class holidaymakers who had taken a Grand Tour of Europe.

The first regatta in England was held in 1775 by the Royal Thames Yacht Club. By 1792 an annual regatta had been established in Whitstable, Kent, and from there (the Napoleonic Wars notwithstanding) races were founded all around the English coastline. An early example of this was the 'maritime event' held at Torbay, Devon, in 1813, which, like these other races, offered trophies to the winners. The event at Torbay became fashionable quickly and attracted

royal patronage from 1828, when the Duchess of Clarence first attended what was by then called 'Torbay Royal Regatta'. Later, in 1839, Queen Victoria came to watch the races.

England's most famous river regatta was founded at Henley-on-Thames in Oxfordshire the same year and was staged with a fair and other amusements. Henley Royal Regatta is still held to this day, offering much-coveted prizes for its amateur races. Since 1851 it has also had royal patronage, with Prince Albert being the first to take on that role and the reigning monarch fulfilling it ever since. Today, Britain's most popular regatta takes place at Cowes, on the Isle of Wight, where typically more than 900 boats take part.

The Sanditon Regatta is a clever idea. It was something relatively new and unusual at the time, which carried with it the glamour of European association and the advantage of a sporting fixture that fitted easily with surrounding social events.

BEHIND THE SCENES

Regatta

Grant Montgomery, the production designer, decided that he wanted to create a lavish outdoor experience for the regatta, which was shot on a lake at Bowood House in Wiltshire. 'There had to be a lot of food. The upper classes in the Regency took servants as their entourage and created extraordinary rooms out of doors. This was an opportunity to have a picnic! Austen mentions lavish feasts in some of her other books, so I was determined to create fruit mountains and jellies – something that would look colourful. I was inspired by drawings of when Napoleon met Tsar Alexander I of Russia and Frederick William III of Prussia at Tilsit. Open-fronted tents, little follies and even rafts.'

SANDITON   **REGATTA**
June 5th,   1819

Entrances for the
MEN'S BOAT RACE
GRAND CHALLENGE CUP.
———ooo———

BRIDPORT BLADES - Mr. T Marston, Mr. S Yates
& Mr. J Radcliffe.

BABINGTON & CROWE - Lord Babington,
Mr. Francis Crowe & Mr. Grey.

THE WORKERS - Mr. James Stringer,
Mr. Fred Robinson, Mr. John Hall.

THE PARKER BROTHERS - Mr. Tom Parker,
Mr. Sidney Parker, Mr. Arthur Parker.

Entrances for the
FISHERMAN'S BOAT RACE.
———ooo———

THE SALTY SEA DOGS - Mr. E. Springer, Mr. S. Yates
& Mr. D. Jennings.

THE BOARMAN BROTHERS - Mr. T Marston,
Mr. S Yates & Mr. J Radcliffe.

REFORMERS - Mr. E Hodges, Mr. R. Stokes,
Mr. M. Harris & Mr. B. Henshaw

SAILOR SISTERS - Mr. R Price, Mr. R. Maddox,
Mr. P. Elton & Mr. W. Price.

Animals on set

The horses and carriages on the *Sanditon* set were provided by the Devil's Horseman, a firm that many of the production team had worked with on other projects. Trainers accompany the horses on set – all Friesian and Hungarian Coldbloods, breeds which were popular in the eighteenth and nineteenth centuries. Some of the animals have special skills. Grant Montgomery, the production designer, explains: 'An individual horse might be trained to fall in a certain way. Say, one animal falls to the left and another one might fall to the right. Or they are trained to rear. So, in one shot we might use a couple of different horses to get the effect we want.' Animal welfare is regulated by law, with set times put aside to rest and feed the horses. Trainers and other experts, like farriers, accompany the animals so any repairs required to horseshoes can be carried out immediately. Shooting days that include horses are always popular with the production team. 'It's just so lovely to see,' one assistant explains. 'The animals are beautiful.'

The carriages were chosen to complement each scene. The curricle driven by Sidney Parker when he first arrives in Sanditon was the Ferrari of its day – a real object of desire. While Tom Parker's brougham coach was customised with his 'TP' logo. For the coach crash that sets the whole story off in the first chapter of Jane Austen's novel, two coaches were used – so that one could be wrecked safely in the scene safely. A wheel was rigged with explosive so that the coach would go over. 'It's all about creating an imaginary world and keeping it fresh,' Grant explains. 'These small details are really important.'

Black Britain

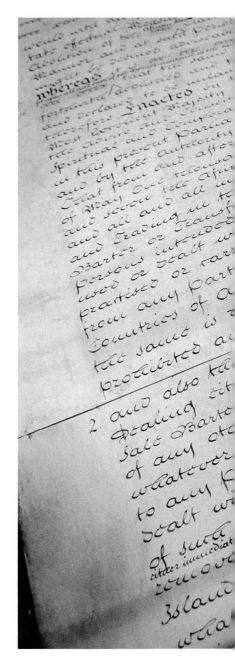

SIDNEY: Georgiana. You know you are worth more than Lady Denham and all her circle put together.

MISS LAMBE: Oh yes. The heiress from the West Indies, rich and black as treacle! Hold her upside down and shake her, hear the sovereigns jingle, a hundred thousand of them! *Episode 2*

In 1819, when this production of *Sanditon* is set, slavery was still legal in British colonies. Slavery on UK soil had been illegal since the twelfth century, though the practice of serfdom was common and (mostly white) serfs working in Scottish coal mines did not conclusively become free until 1799. Though British air was said to be 'too pure an air for a slave to breathe', there is evidence of black African slaves being bought and sold on English soil illegally in the early eighteenth century, and it was not until 1772, when a landmark case ruled that a fugitive black slave from Virginia called James Somersett could not be forced to return to the US, that it was established that black people enslaved elsewhere had freedom of movement in English law.

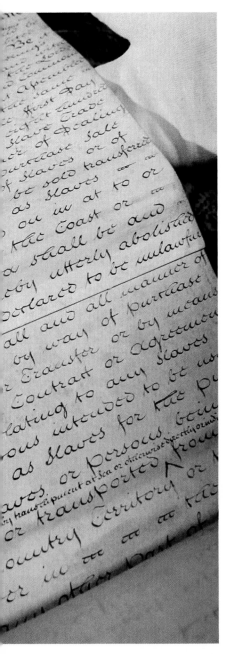

*Above: The original 1806 Foreign
Slave Trade Abolition Bill.*

Forty years after that landmark ruling, the 1807 Slave Trade Act made the trafficking of slaves illegal in British law. This was enforced by the Royal Navy, which stopped not only British ships but the vessels of other nations, where it could, to try to end the industry. The act, however, did not put an end to the ownership of slaves in British colonies and elsewhere. At this time, it is estimated that there were 4 million black slaves in the southern states of America. Because slavery did not exist in the UK (and Britain's role in establishing the slave trade was largely ignored), like Charlotte many people in England who had heard about the act thought that slavery itself had been abolished and was no longer a problem. We know that Jane Austen, however, supported full abolition and so presumably was aware that slavery still existed elsewhere.

Member of Parliament William Wilberforce, who brought forward the Slave Trade Act, continued to campaign to free all slaves. His political arguments were underlined by several slave uprisings and rebellions in the colonies during the period and real-life accounts written mostly by freed black slaves. However, there was huge opposition to the abolition movement. The pro-slavery West Indian lobby included powerful voices: they contended that banning slavery would cause the UK economy to collapse and also put forward a Bible-based argument that God intended black people to live as slaves. Several churches had invested in plantations and they added their weight to the case against freeing enslaved people, but the abolitionists continued what was to become a long and difficult battle. Slavery was not finally abolished across the British Empire until 1833.

There is evidence of black people living in the UK from as far back as Roman times. Analysis of DNA from skeletons in Roman graves in London confirmed twenty-two individuals buried there had come from Africa. This is not surprising: North Africa was Romanised at this time and was multiethnic. These skeletons probably belonged to free men in the Roman army (and potentially their wives). In medieval times there is some evidence of black Africans coming to Britain after the Crusades, and in medieval Scotland there is documentary evidence of black servants and entertainers working at the Scottish royal court, including a poem written to one of the women by a Scottish nobleman. By the eighteenth century it is estimated there was a small population of about 10,000 black people in the UK, most of them living in London. After the American War of Independence, this number was augmented by a few hundred black loyalists who came to settle in Britain. The anti-slavery lobby included several educated and eloquent black abolitionists. These people campaigned vigorously, organising meetings, writing pamphlets and books, and adding weight to the cause with their own stories. One was Olaudah Equiano, a former slave, who wrote a memoir of his life that became a bestseller – *The Interesting Narrative of the Life of Olaudah Equiano*. He was the first black person to be employed by the British government, when in 1786 he became commissary of provisions and stores for 350 black people living in poverty who were deported to Sierra Leone.

There is no question that Britain in the Regency era was institutionally racist. Today, the language used around black and mixed-race people sounds shocking to the modern ear, as are many of the assumptions made by Britain's white politicians and commentators of the era. However, the abolitionists prevailed by slowly but surely winning over public

William Wilberforce.

'Necessity is the plea for every infringement of human freedom. It is the argument of tyrants; it is the creed of slaves.'

William Pitt the Younger

opinion, and by the 1830s the majority of people had come out against slavery, at least.

Black heiresses like Georgiana Lambe were unusual but not unheard of. Some white plantation owners recognised and/or married their black partners (who were mostly slaves) and legitimised their mixed-race children. These children could then inherit. Another group of black people who came to Britain were freed slaves who had made their own fortune. One such was Doll Thomas, known as the 'Queen of Demerara', who arrived in Glasgow in August 1810 to arrange a British education for some of her grandchildren. Doll was fabulously wealthy – when she visited London it is said she wore a necklace made of doubloons (gold coins) and a skirt made of five-pound notes. Like many wealthy free black people, Doll also owned slaves herself and was compensated like all slave owners for her loss when slavery was finally abolished.

'Those who deny freedom to others, deserve it not themselves'

Abraham Lincoln

Olaudah Equiano.

GEORGIANA LAMBE
Crystal Clarke

———

SIDNEY PARKER:
You mistake me: I have your interests very much at heart.

MISS LAMBE:
Then you should have left me where you found me.

SIDNEY PARKER:
Believe me, I wish I could have, but duty dictated otherwise.

MISS LAMBE:
Damn your duty.

– Episode 1

———

*'Miss Lambe has an immense fortune – richer than all
the others – and very delicate health.'*

SANDITON

INTERVIEW

Georgiana Lambe, played by Crystal Clarke

Wilful and headstrong, Georgiana is grieving the loss of her father and her subsequent removal from Antigua, her home. An heiress with £100,000 to her name at only nineteen years of age, she is aware that she is a high prize on the marriage market and hates the attention this brings her. Her black heritage also makes her a focus of gossip – an uncomfortable position in a small town. Georgiana is frustrated with the restrictions of being Sidney's ward, hates being treated as a curiosity, and feels both these things more deeply than she would generally admit.

How were you first introduced to Jane Austen's work?

Clueless was one of my favourite films when I was a kid. I didn't know, growing up, that it was an adaptation of Emma *but, when I found out, I suppose that introduced Austen to me. I also loved Emma Thompson's* Sense and Sensibility *– the fact she wrote the script and then acted in it is great.*

Georgiana's ideas about romance are very clear. What advice would you give her?

Follow your heart, but don't forget your head.

As a black woman, was this an important part for you to play?

Without a doubt. Many people don't know about the presence of people of colour in the UK prior to the mid-twentieth century. This part gives a fuller picture of history and Georgiana can give a voice to some of those people.

How does playing period drama differ from other contemporary roles?
The characters aren't as direct – they can be quite passive-aggressive. It's all about the side-eye!

What would you do if you were a massively wealthy heiress?
I'm inspired by Angela Davis of the Black Panther Party. I'd put money into something like that – counterculture politics to combat racism. And go shopping, of course!

Georgiana has some fabulous outfits. Is there anything from her wardrobe you'd wear in real life?
The yellow pelisse coat Georgiana wore on the beach when she was painting. It's beautiful. I'd wear that in a heartbeat.

· • • • ·

Etiquette

It was believed in the Regency era that the upper classes had an inbuilt sense of decorum. This was probably the result of being brought up in an upper-class environment rather than anything nature could endow, and was known as being 'well bred' rather than being 'well brought up'. Manners were considered hugely important and were dictated by a complex set of rules known as etiquette.

A well-bred person moved gracefully and maintained a calm assurance. This was considered dignified rather than standoffish. Etiquette was designed to keep people you didn't know at arm's length and curtail any inappropriate familiarity.

A formal introduction was required before talking to somebody you didn't know. This would usually be undertaken by the head of the household or the host at a social event. Once you were introduced, a woman would incline and give a slight curtsey, and a gentleman would bow, just as you see in *Sanditon* when Charlotte is introduced into society in the town. This practice would continue for the rest of the acquaintanceship – it was considered extremely rude not to greet people to whom you had been introduced when you ran into them again. This was known as 'cutting' somebody. You didn't have to speak to everyone you met – it was simply expected that you would

'For a working-class man like James Stringer to win Charlotte he needs a special something that shines through – a truthfulness and kindness that she can identify with.'

Leo Suter, playing
Young Stringer

'Fan Flirtation' by Henry Gillard
Glindoni, 1908.

acknowledge an acquaintance with a nod of the head at least.

In conversation the etiquette was not to ask personal questions, and gossip was forbidden. Touching was also kept to a minimum between acquaintances. Address was always formal; if you used somebody's first name, it meant you had become intimate with them and, in fact, this is a development we see in Charlotte's relationship with Georgiana – they call each other by their first names as soon as they become confidantes. For many people, they would spend years never using their friends' first names, and it was not uncommon for women to become engaged to their future husbands without deviating from the 'proper' formal forms of address. The worst trespass was to be vulgar – you could be forgiven almost anything else.

To develop a friendship, first you would call on an acquaintance. This usually happened in the afternoon and initially most calls would not last more than half an hour. If the person wasn't in, you might leave a calling card to show that you had come to visit them. In the country, where matters were generally less formal, it was acceptable for a lower-class person to call on a superior if they were new to the area, but in town things were more constrained. Men received callers in their library or study and women received callers in the morning or drawing rooms.

At a dinner party, guests would enter the dining room in order of precedence – that is, according to their title and station. Higher-ranking guests would sit closer to the host and hostess (who took their seats at opposite ends of the table), with everyone else finding their own place in between. At a formal dinner you would usually only speak to the two people on either side of you – talking 'cross table' was not acceptable unless it was a more informal party. Women were encouraged not to display an appetite by eating too enthusiastically, which suggested either that they were hungry (heaven forfend) or that they could not control themselves. Servants were always ignored at mealtimes. At the end of the meal the hostess would signal everybody to rise. Women would then withdraw for tea and leave the men at the table to drink port and smoke cigars.

In courtship, women were likewise not expected to show too much enthusiasm and could not overtly be seen to pursue a man's attention. That was up to the fellows!

SIR EDWARD DENHAM
Jack Fox

CLARA:

He is not to be trusted – and you should be on your guard against him too. I say this as your friend. He has no conscience and no sense of what is proper or decent. I believe he intends to ruin me in Lady Denham's eyes.

CHARLOTTE:

How shocking. But why should he do that?

CLARA:

Because she favours me, of course. He fears she will favour me over him in her will. But he sees every girl he encounters as fair game.

LADY DENHAM:

Yes, he is very well to look at, very pleasing to the young ladies, and no doubt he'll sow some wild oats – but he must marry for money.

– Episode 1

'Sir Edward's great object in life was to be seductive. With such personal advantages as he knew himself to possess, and such talents as he did also give himself credit for, he regarded it as his duty.'

NARRATOR, *SANDITON*

Sir Edward Denham, played by Jack Fox

Lady Denham's nephew Sir Edward hopes to secure the old lady's inheritance along with his stepsister Esther. Although he has a title and a healthy ego to go with it, he does not have much money at his disposal, so it is very important that he marries well – to someone with as much money as possible. He considers Sanditon a backwater and is only there to try to gain Lady Denham's favour – and there is very little he will not do to achieve this. Edward's relationship with his stepsister is intimate and inappropriate – like a delicious poison.

Edward's character is all about money and privilege. Do you feel he is amoral?

We all learn to survive in the environment we live in and Edward has to do that too. He thinks money will solve everything and that money can buy everything. He's got the ignorance of youth.

What did you learn from *Sanditon* about where Britain comes from?

It's such a rich history. The Regency is so Roman, so it goes even further back to the days when empire was a good thing. It's like before the fall – when pride is at its peak.

What do you like about the Regency look?

The velvet collars and the boots! They're timeless.

Those scenes with Charlotte Spencer are full of creepy sexuality. Was shooting them difficult?

It's all about getting into the mind of the character. I think Edward likes the discomfort of it. It brings out the truth, somehow, like catching someone off guard so they will tell you the truth.

Do you prefer small screen or big screen?

The big screen is becoming the small screen and with TV you get a big arc in the story – you can show so much more.

What advice would you give Edward?

Life has a way of testing you, so be prepared to learn that if you do the crime, you'll do the time.

Debt

Debt was a day-to-day fact of Regency life. Most middle- and upper-class families ran accounts with all kinds of suppliers, for which the men in the family were responsible. Married women, who were not legal entities, could not be prosecuted for debt (in fact, their husbands were held entirely responsible for any spending that their wives and daughters undertook). The upper classes were commonly profligate, running up large gambling debts at sporting events or at cards – money matters were often considered 'sordid' and beneath them. As a result, businesses could suffer huge cash-flow problems as upper-class customers simply ignored their bills until they felt like paying.

The reality of Regency life meant that it was costly to pursue a debtor and if payments were consistently not made, it was common for several tradesmen to band together to pay for a writ to get their money. When this happened the man charged was held in a halfway house to give him time to settle up. If after that his debts caught up with him and he was declared bankrupt, he could be sent to prison. Unscrupulous creditors would often pursue their debt well beyond the law, issuing threats of physical violence.

Sticking with the legal route to recovery, in London there were three dedicated prisons for debtors, but if these were full or too far away, those convicted for debt could simply

be incarcerated in a regular jail. If it went that far, it was difficult for a man to clear his name. Once inside, you couldn't work and had to try to raise money via friends and family to pay your debts, which had to be fully discharged before you could be released. There are records that show men still in prison for outstanding debts of a mere 4d (pence), and in 1803 a study revealed that fewer than one in ten debtors managed to make their way out of jail, back to their families.

For the family the situation was also near impossible. With the main earner (or money-manager) locked up, word would spread quickly and all lines of credit would abruptly stop. Upper- and middle-class women and their children were left stranded socially, selling anything they could to raise money to live on as well as to offset their family's debt. It's no wonder that some debtors simply fled abroad with their families, where they could not be pursued, leaving creditors to mop up the mess. In a few cases, where the debtor might have particular skills useful to them, the Royal Navy paid off debts and the debtor was then pressed into naval service.

Inner Court, Fleet Prison, London.

· • • ·

The value of money

In the Regency period money was expressed as guineas, pounds, shillings and pence.

☞ **A guinea was worth 1 pound and 1 shilling, and was an upmarket way of expressing prices.**

☞ **A pound was worth 20 shillings, or 240 pence.**

☞ **A crown was worth 5 shillings or 60 pence.**

☞ **A shilling was 12 pence.**

☞ **A halfpenny was just that – half a penny – though it was usually called a 'ha'penny'.**

☞ **A farthing was a quarter-penny.**

At the time *Sanditon* is set, wages were low – very little premium was put on a working-class person's time. A male household servant might earn up to £25 a year (often less) and a female household servant could earn up to £12 a year. An ordinary sailor would earn between these two amounts – around £16 annually. All these workers usually had accommodation and board included as part of their employment package – in the house where they worked or onboard ship.

'What have wealth or grandeur to do with happiness?'

Elinor Dashwood,
Sense and Sensibility

From left to right – farthing, half penny, penny, three pence, six pence, one shilling, two shillings, half crown and coronation crown.

Some skills were valued more highly – and the rewards of such jobs had to cover the person's living expenses independently. A tailor could expect to earn around £70 a year and a good clerk around £150 annually. Roles that came with responsibility for staff were rewarded even better. The captain of a ship in the Royal Navy (in charge of an entire crew) might make around £250 a year.

Though these annual wages don't sound like a lot of money, the prices of goods were also cheaper. Still, some common items were more expensive proportionally than they are today. So, for example, beef cost 6d (pence) a pound – a larger portion of a daily wage than it would be today; whereas bread was a ha'penny for a quarter-loaf – relatively cheap. For this reason, it's difficult sometimes to understand the value of money in the Regency era (or in Jane Austen's novels). Not only is the money worth less than today, it also buys different goods. As a ready reckoner, £1 in 1812 is worth around £340 today.

Some things were out of the reach of ordinary people. A decent riding horse (not top of the range) cost £20 – more than most unskilled or low-skilled workers earned in a year. A really top-quality horse would set you back seventy guineas and was the preserve of the gentleman. Luxury household items like a piano cost £34. To put this in perspective, Jane Austen herself had an allowance in the final years of her father's life of £40 a year to cover clothes and personal costs (not living expenses).

CHARLOTTE HEYWOOD
Rose Williams

CHARLOTTE:
You have no need to explain yourself to me.

SIR EDWARD:
But – you promise you won't speak of it to others?

CHARLOTTE:
Do you really think I would?

SIR EDWARD:
No, of course – you are altogether too good, too pure in heart to gossip.

– Episode 1

'She was a very sober-minded young lady, sufficiently well read in novels to supply her imagination with amusement.'

Narrator, *Sanditon*

Charlotte Heywood, played by Rose Williams

Charlotte, at twenty-two, comes to Sanditon after a chance encounter with Tom and Mary Parker at her family home in Willingden, after which they invite her to stay for the season. The attractive daughter of a well-heeled farmer, Charlotte is socially inferior to most of the other characters, but she is bright and good-natured and has a sense of fair play and a cool head in a crisis. She fits in well at the new resort.

When you were first cast, were you excited?

Honestly, I couldn't believe it. It's such an honour and the production is so exciting. It feels like such a fresh story.

What does it feel like being a Regency woman?

It's very elegant! Playing an historical role really makes you think about where you come from – culturally I mean. I love that.

Did you blush having to do the nude scene with Theo?

Yes, though I should say – he was wearing a modesty pouch!

What was the scariest aspect of Regency life?

For me it was realising that as a woman you were basically just a piece of property. You had no rights and were completely reliant on the men around you. It makes you so vulnerable.

Which item of *Sanditon* costume would you like to wear in real life?

My mother worked in a costume department and I used to help out there, so the clothes are really important to me. The sand-coloured coat that I wear in the opening episode is my favourite. It looks like a designer item and the colour is a bridge between the earthy brown tones of the country and the lighter, brighter colours at the seaside.

Bathing in the sea is cold, right?

Oh my God, yes. The crew was wonderful that day. We needed lots of takes and we were all in the water for ages. I was wearing a dry suit underneath my clothes and I still got completely frozen.

· • • • ·

Fashion for women

ALISON: What about this one?

CHARLOTTE: Oh, I don't know . . .
everything is so old and out of fashion . . . I
think I have nothing that will do.   *Episode 1*

*'. . . man only can be aware
of the insensibility of man
towards a new gown . . .
Woman is fine for her
satisfaction alone. No man
will admire her the more,
no woman will like her
the better for it.'*

Narrator, *Northanger Abbey*

Clothes for women changed dramatically during the
Regency era, becoming inspired by classical fashion from
Greek and Roman times. Draping was important to this
look, which was a marked change from earlier eighteenth-
century styles where women wore complex, heavily corseted
dresses with skirts so wide that they could not walk through
a door without turning sideways. By contrast, the classic
Regency look is a simple one-piece dress with a high waist.
It was acceptable for women to show bare arms and have
relatively low-cut tops, which allowed them to show off
necklaces and other accessories. This was a pretty look that
could be easily added to with a wrap, a bonnet, a pair of
gloves and, of course, a fan. Accessories could be an expensive business and middle- and upper-class women were
usually given an annual allowance to spend on clothes
and personal items, like Austen's own £40 annual allowance. After the social upheaval of the French Revolution,

there was a sense that fashion had become too complex and there was a general desire to return to something more simple.

DRESSES

In the early Regency, dresses were always referred to as 'gowns', but the term 'frocks' later became fashionable. Muslin was the most popular fabric in the early nineteenth century for dresses. This is light, drapes beautifully and was often left undyed and worn white. The burgeoning industry in automated spinning, weaving and cotton-printing of fabrics meant that material was less expensive than in previous decades, and the first sewing machines (launched in 1814) meant that it became cheaper and easier to make clothes. This is the classic look of the era – short-sleeved, high-waisted with lots of draping. Lace was also fashionable: a visitor to Bowood House (where the regatta scenes in *Sanditon* was filmed) remarked in 1809 that the ladies of the party were wearing 'more profusion of lace than anything my countrified imagination could have conceived'.

When the classic Regency look first emerged it was considered daring for a lady to have so much flesh on show. Women of all classes sewed their own clothes, with middle- and upper-class women also employing dressmakers who had their own premises, or might visit the household to take measurements and hold fittings. When this style was launched the aim was to look like a statue that had come to life – part of the classical vogue. As one contemporary observer commented: 'Everything we now use is made in

'*I like the Gown very much & my Mother thinks it very ugly.*'

Jane Austen to Cassandra Austen, October 1800

imitation of those models lately discovered in Italy.' Over the decades of the Regency the look became more complicated, and into the 1820s waistlines dropped and corsets came back into fashion.

THE PELISSE

Over her dress, to stay warm, a lady would wear either a 'spencer' or a 'pelisse' – the first is a fitted jacket very like a gentleman's tailcoat, but without the tails; the longer pelisse is a buttoned-up coat that echoed the shape of Regency high-waisted, long-sleeved dresses. Pelisses were commonly made with velvet but could be run up using other materials. The pelisse was based on a military design and early in the era usually had braid adornments and was edged with fur. But as the Regency wore on these embellishments fell out of fashion, though the shape of the pelisse remained and was widely worn – especially in winter when women still donned muslin dresses, despite the cold.

UNDERWEAR

Under a dress a lady would always wear a chemise, which was a simple cotton shift that looks like a nightdress. The chemise stopped the muslin dress being see-through – like a modern-day slip. Sometimes women added a short top (also usually in cotton) called a chemisette. The rim of the chemisette showed over the top of the dress neckline. Then 'stays', or corsets, could be added to raise and enhance the line of the breasts. These were not Victorian corsets, which were far less flexible. Not all women wore them. In addition, not all women wore pants (or drawers, as they were known) and, when they did, these were constructed out of two legs (like plus-fours) that attached at the top with ties (like laces) – so they were crotchless. This meant that women did not have to 'undress' in order to go to the bathroom and could simply squat. The addition of a petticoat, usually made out of a stiffer fabric, on top of all this gave dresses an added flounce and made the outfit warmer.

BONNETS

A bonnet finished an outfit and many women enjoyed trimming these themselves, though there were specialist hatters who could be employed to make one for you. Turbans were also popular and considered extremely smart and exotic. Trimmings might include embroidery, crochet or feathers, with flower and fruit motifs. Married women usually wore a mob, lace or draped cap, even indoors. Unmarried women tended to simply dress their hair, only donning a hat if they were going out. Hats were a mark of respect – no decent woman would attend church without wearing one.

SHOES

Often made out of silk or delicate leather, ladies' shoes were not hardy. While walking was a popular activity, these shoes (which came in various shapes, from the slipper to the high heel) were really only for show. Working-class women wore thick leather boots (or if they were very poor, no shoes at all)

'I cannot determine what to do about my new Gown; I wish such things were to be bought ready made.'

Jane Austen to Cassandra Austen, December 1798

I am determined to buy a handsome [muslin Gown] whenever I can, & am so tired & ashamed of half my present stock that I even blush at the sight of the wardrobe that contains them.'

Jane Austen to Cassandra Austen, December 1798

and a lady might keep a pair of these to hand if she liked walking in the countryside and did not want to keep to the path, like Lizzie Bennet in *Pride and Prejudice*.

Shoes were often made by hand and fitted individually. Charlotte's delight on spotting pre-made blue-satin shoes she loves in a shop window in Sanditon is understandable – she has come from the countryside and a place where there would have been few social engagements, and the shoes symbolise the elegant world she is excited about joining.

ACCESSORIES

Accessories like parasols (to keep off the sun), fans and shawls were highly prized. Many of these were imported, from Europe and further afield – for example, from China and India, where British companies had been trading successfully for decades. Limerick gloves came into fashion in the mid-1700s and remained popular. These were extremely fine long leather gloves. The design came from an Irish glovemaker, Cornelius Lyon. The finest ones were made from the skins of unborn calves and could be rolled up to fit inside a large walnut shell.

THE RETICULE

Ladies commonly carried a small bag or 'reticule' to carry money, a handkerchief and other items they wanted to take with them. Reticules usually had a drawstring to close them and could be embroidered or trimmed with pretty ribbons.

BEHIND THE SCENES

Wardrobe

Walking into the costume department on the *Sanditon* set, it feels like a hive of industry. The core team consists of eleven people, with extra hands called in for days when crowd scenes were filming. Sam Perry, the production's costume designer, says, 'The team are amazing. Everyone really pulls together and works hard. We usually start at six thirty in the morning, but on busy days everybody is in by five thirty. There is always something to be done.' The department consists of rack upon rack of itemised clothing, which is stored on set and often loaded onto trucks for location shoots. Every character, from the principal actor with the largest role to the briefest extra, is fitted individually and the laundry is also done in the department.

Sam started to plan the wardrobe only a few weeks before filming started. 'They told me I had got the job and I started the same day,' she says. 'It took six weeks to take on the rest of the crew, do the research, plan what we'd need for each scene and source it.' Many of the costumes were hired from specialists but the team also commissioned some pieces. 'I had some of the ballgowns made – Miss Lambe's teal duchess satin dress and Esther's deep maroon silk ballgown were both commissioned specially for the ball,' Sam says. 'It's surprisingly expensive to clothe a ball – we have seventy supporting artists and eighteen principals and that takes a lot of clothes and accessories. For example, we needed forty pairs of men's shoes alone.'

Sam felt it was important to commission some workaday pieces, too. The main cast members all had shoes and boots made to order. 'Young Stringer's boots were an interesting job. We wanted the actor to be comfortable, so they had to fit exactly, but he's working class and his clothes would have been worn, so we broke down the boots, using graters and sandpaper to make them look older.' Sam also commissioned several hats, including a stern riding hat for Esther Denham. 'That was important,' Sam said. 'She's such a strict character and I wanted to distinguish her – give her a different silhouette.'

It's not only the outerwear that is important: female actors wear chemises, petticoats, silk petticoats and a bodice underneath each outfit – just as real Regency women would have done. 'The men only wear a cotton or linen shift under their clothes,' Sam explains, 'and for nude scenes we provide them with modesty pouches made of flesh-coloured Lycra. The swimming scenes were a real challenge – we had to try to keep everyone warm, so we got dry suits and then designed what the actors would wear on top so they couldn't be seen. For the ladies that meant high-necked cotton smocks, which had to be weighted down to stop them floating. For the female attendants who manned the bathing machines it meant layer upon layer of thermals.'

· • • ·

Fashion for men

There was a sea change in upper-class menswear during the Regency era. Out with fussy powdered wigs and ornately decorated frock coats and in with clear, classic lines, short hair and muted colours. This movement started in France (which influenced British fashion), where more sober styles of dress had been adopted after the French Revolution as a way of rejecting feudalism. However, in Britain, the changes were also allied to the fact that this look was more in line with military clothing, which provided inspiration during the time the country was at war (ironically with France). As mechanisation made decoration easier and cheaper, the middle and upper classes also moved away from heavy brocades and fringing, which were no longer status symbols.

The personification of Regency menswear came in the form of the 'dandy'. Dandies were well-dressed, fashionable men who prided themselves on being commentators on both society and culture. The most famous dandy of the Regency era was Beau Brummell (George Bryan Brummell), who was the poster boy for the classic Regency men's look of dark, well-cut fitted clothes. Brummell had been an officer in the 10th Royal Hussars and had broken his nose in a riding accident. He was part of the Prince of Wales's circle – he had probably known the prince since his schooldays at

Beau Brummell.

'To be truly elegant one should not be noticed.'

Beau Brummell

Eton. Brummell usually wore a dark cutaway cloth tailcoat with brass buttons and a standing collar, a plain waistcoat that matched his pantaloons (shorter breeches had fallen out of fashion around 1805), hessian riding boots (which were military in nature) and a hard conical riding hat. It is said he took over an hour to tie his cravat and five hours to get dressed completely (a feat which could only be achieved with the help of his valet). In the evening, Brummell might wear a black coat and silk pantaloons. It became a custom among the fashionable set to arrive at Brummell's house on Chesterfield Street in Mayfair every morning just to see him dress.

Brummell was an obsessive – he recommended polishing leather boots with champagne – and it is no wonder that he ran up huge debts and ended up fleeing the country in 1816, having worked his way through a £30,000 inheritance and borrowed tens of thousands of pounds more. He was extremely unpopular in some quarters because he was conceited and had a very sharp tongue. He is famously said to have insulted the Prince Regent, asking a mutual acquaintance, 'Who is your fat friend?' For many years, however, he was one of the regent's favourites because of his undoubted style and wit; though in the end the prince took offence at Brummell's repeated rudeness. Some in society still loved him, however, and when he ended up in debtors' prison in France, money was sent from England to bail him out and have him housed in a charitable asylum in Caen, where the Duchess of York (said to have been his lover) sent a comfortable chair to furnish his room. He died, probably of syphilis, in France in 1840.

While dandies spent a huge amount of effort choosing outerwear, men in this period didn't wear underwear – there

'Starch makes the gentleman, etiquette the lady.'

Beau Brummell

was thought to be no need as their clothes were neither see-through nor likely to fly up in the wind. Pantaloons were fastened with a button fly at the front to allow the wearer to use a chamber pot easily. At night men wore a simple shift – like a nightshirt. In addition to the tailcoat, an overcoat would be donned in colder weather, usually with a fancy collar of fur or velvet. One popular style was known as the Garrick and had a cape attached to the collar.

Accessories were vital: gloves, canes and pocket watches were important parts of an outfit. Most men carried a snuff box, which would usually have been made from silver, sometimes with enamel decoration. These were objects of desire. Beau Brummell famously hid his snuff box from the Prince Regent, afraid that his friend would take it. Shoes with buckles fell from favour in the Regency era and, if not wearing boots, gentlemen might don laced-up leather shoes, usually black, over silk or cotton stockings. To top off their outfit, a gentleman would always wear a hat – by 1815 top hats were coming into fashion and in winter might be lined with fur. They were sometimes collapsible for easy storage.

Working men did not partake in the high fashion of Regency society. In the country many continued to wear breeches as they had always done and were unable to afford the expensive tailoring required for tailcoats with standing collars and the distinctive Regency 'M' cut into the lapel. The tricorn hat, which had fallen out of fashion among the upper classes, continued to be worn by the working classes for far longer. In *Sanditon*, Young Stringer and the other workmen cannot afford fancy fabrics, but their clothes are more comfortable and easier to move around in. It was common practice for the upper classes to pass on clothes

'No perfumes, he used to say, but very fine linen, plenty of it, and country washing.'

Captain Jesse, biographer of Beau Brummell

to their servants when they had tired of them. This meant that people in service were among the snappier dressers of the working class. Where men worked in a household, particularly in roles where they would be seen by guests, their clothes would be provided by their employer, and because this reflected the household's taste and style often footmen and butlers were provided with high-quality outfits. An employer often had a set 'livery', which comprised particular colours and fabrics from which all uniforms were made for their household staff. This is similar to a jockey wearing an owner's colours today.

> *'Vanity and pride are different things, though the words are often used synonymously. A person may be proud without vain. Pride relates more to our opinion of ourselves, vanity to what we would have others think of us.'*
>
> Mary Bennett, *Pride and Prejudice*

6
HEALTH

· • • ·

ARTHUR: I like the air, you know, as much as anyone, but it doesn't like me. My nerves, you know. My sister thinks me bilious, but I doubt it. If I were bilious, wine would disagree with me, but it always does my nerves good. Do you know, the more I drink, the better I feel. I often wake up in the morning feeling very groggy, but after a few glasses of wine I'm right as rain! That is quite remarkable, don't you think?   *Episode 1*

TOM PARKER: I do not like to contradict you, ma'am –

LADY DENHAM: Then don't!

TOM PARKER: But the fact of the matter is – you cannot have a seaside resort without a doctor. And there is no one more qualified than Dr Fuchs.   *Episode 2*

· • • • ·

Medical men

I N *SANDITON,* **HEALTH** is a main theme – seaside resorts, after all, became attractive during the Regency because of their health benefits. But what could you expect in terms of health care during this period?

Becoming a doctor, like Dr Fuchs, was largely unregulated. Until very close to the era when *Sanditon* is set, it had been easy to start as a medical man and simply start practising. That is not to say that medical schools didn't exist. Many colleges were connected to large hospitals – like St Bartholomew's Hospital and Guy's Hospital in London. Here, student doctors could take a course that might last anything from a year to upwards of three years and was extremely hands-on. Patients, by the time they got to hospitals, were almost always extremely ill, so doctors who undertook this kind of training didn't gain much experience in mild ailments – the day-to-day medical issues that most of a GP's clients might bring to his surgery. It was also common for younger doctors to be apprenticed to more established practitioners – in what we'd now think of as GP practices. The poet John Keats became just such an apprentice at the age of sixteen, qualifying two years later in 1814 and setting up on his own as a surgeon.

Keats got in just under the wire. In 1815 the law changed and all doctors were required to attend proper medical

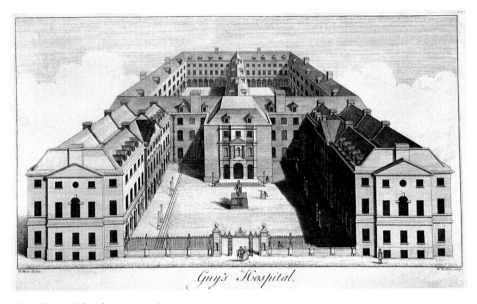

Guy's Hospital.

Guy's Hospital, London, circa 1756.

schools and pass exams to qualify – in fact, Keats went on to do exactly that, qualifying as an apothecary in 1816 after training for a further six months. There were different levels of medical training available – you could become an apothecary (or pharmacist) as Keats chose to do. This meant you could make and dispense medicine (like chemists do today). For the poor, the apothecary would be the first port of the call when they were ill – simply buying remedies over the counter. In country areas without a doctor (like Sanditon before Dr Fuchs arrives) an apothecary would fulfil the function of medical adviser for everyone in the community.

A wide spectrum of traditional herbal remedies was available. *Culpeper's Complete Herbal* (first published in 1653) was kept in many homes and its recipes were made up by apothecaries. Many of these cures were effective for complaints such as kidney problems, bruising, jaundice, eye infections, ulcers, boils, diarrhoea, colic or the healing of wounds. Some are still in use today, such as clove oil for toothache or Epsom salts taken as an antacid to aid digestion. Others were dangerous – like 'grey powder', which was made from chalk and mercury (highly poisonous) and used as a purgative. Use of laudanum (what we would call opium) was widespread as a painkiller and was highly addictive.

The next step up from the apothecary, as a student of medicine was to train to become a surgeon. This was akin to being a junior doctor and did not always mean you would undertake operations. Surgery was a terrible experience in the early nineteenth century. There was no anaesthetic – patients were commonly forced to drink quantities of hard spirits to dull the pain, after which they would be held or tied down for the procedure. The surgery itself often took place in a lecture theatre or hall with students in attendance. These halls were not sterile environments; in fact, dissections took place on the same operating tables without much in the way of cleaning taking place between the dissection of a dead body and surgery – or even two surgeries on different people. Only what would now be considered very basic operations were possible: amputations and the removal of obvious growths like goitres. The doctor performing the surgery worked extremely quickly (they had to because of the pain involved) and this meant that mistakes were common. It was far more important to get a gangrenous leg off swiftly than it was to do so tidily. Around twenty-five per cent of patients died from post-surgical infections in this era.

At the top of the medical tree, if you qualified as a physician, you could diagnose cases, perform surgeries and take further exams to become a 'consulting physician', which meant that other doctors might ask you to advise on tricky

Mr NICHOLAS CULPEPER.

Milk Thistle

Chamomile

Culpeper's Complete Herbal, *1653*.

Echinacea

Saffron

cases. You were only allowed to give yourself the title 'Dr' if you had qualified to the level of physician or consulting physician, although both surgeons and doctors undertook surgery. Dr Fuchs is fully qualified and during the course of the series gives some good advice (especially to Arthur and Diana Parker who are not ill, only overindulged). Where he prescribes ineffective treatments (like his water bath) he is absolutely in line with the medical thinking of the day.

Georgian doctors understood anatomy – dissection was a routine part of their training – but the details of how human anatomy worked were hazy. Very little was known about biochemistry or endocrinology, and medical understanding was centred around the ancient system of 'humours' of the body – the concept that there were 'vital forces' which ran the nervous and blood/bone marrow systems. It was believed that these vital forces were limited and needed to be balanced, so disease might be put down to expending too much mental energy, which, it was then thought, depleted physical energy. Or the other way around. Water- or airborne diseases were not understood. If you got ill, it was believed to be either because of your genetic make-up (called 'inherited susceptibility' by Georgian doctors), your lifestyle (which knocked the humours out of joint) or your environment (get thee to the seaside – hence the rise of resorts like Sanditon in the era). Rest was the cure most often prescribed.

Doctors used their own bodies as sounding boards for illness. They'd check their own pulse before the patient's and judge from that whether the 'blood was running too quickly'. Doctors shared their observations and theories with each other in widely available medical journals, and papers were also presented at the Royal Society in London.

INOCULATION

Inoculation became a common practice over the course of the eighteenth and early nineteenth centuries. The details and success of the method were shared in journals and discussed by gatherings of medical men, who then went on to recommend the practice to their clients. While measles, mumps and rubella were not yet inoculated against, smallpox (now almost eradicated) was first inoculated against in Britain during the 1720s by a process called variolation. This practice was brought back from Istanbul by Lady Mary Wortley Montagu, who had herself suffered from the disease and also lost a brother to it. While it was effective, a certain percentage of patients who undertook the procedure died or went on to develop the full disease. In 1796 local doctor Edward Jenner ran experiments using the less dangerous cowpox to inoculate against smallpox and coined the word 'vaccination' (from the Latin *vacca*, which means 'cow'). By 1800 the practice was becoming commonplace in Britain and was 'exported' to mainland Europe and America. Such was Jenner's contribution to public health that he received £10,000 from the government in 1802 and a further £20,000 in 1807.

Edward Jenner also wrote about his theories on the subject of heart disease, which he believed was due to constriction of the arteries – an impressive precursor to modern cardiology.

ADVANCING KNOWLEDGE

Another Regency advance was in the fight against scurvy. In the 1740s a Scottish ship's doctor, James Lind, undertook an experiment over the course of a voyage, feeding sailors citrus fruit against five other control groups (one of which had to drink a measure of seawater daily). The results were noted and, while the Royal Navy did not make the prescription of vitamin C regulation until over forty years later, Lind wrote up his discovery in a treatise in 1753 and the information was shared among the medical community. As a result, it was possible to reduce scurvy-related mortality and illness from levels that often ran at over fifty per cent of the crew on long voyages. By the Regency, it was more common for sailors

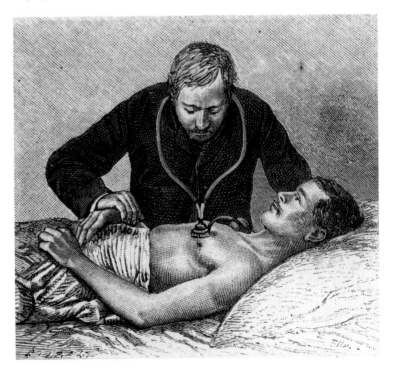

Dr Constantin Paul using the
Galante stethoscope, circa 1885.

to die (like all men during the period) from accidents at work than it was from disease. In a strange aside, seamen who ate rats they had caught aboard the ship were also protected from scurvy, as rats can manufacture their own vitamin C – though Lind did not make this connection or understand about the rats. He thought the acidity of the fruit he prescribed was what made it effective. Vitamins and their specific health benefits were not discovered until well into the twentieth century.

This is a common theme when considering medicine within the period – again and again doctors notice that something is effective and adopt certain practices because they are successful, but they don't understand why the remedy works.

The Regency era also saw advances in medical equipment; many doctors, like Dr Fuchs, were engaged in experimenting in this field, some with more success than others. In 1816 a French doctor, René Théophile-Hyacinthe Laennec, invented the stethoscope. Doctors had amplified the sound of the heartbeat by means of rolling up a newspaper for decades, but Théophile-Hyacinthe Laennec was the first to make an instrument to do the job. He went on to mass-produce it. The stethoscope quickly became part of every Regency doctor's kit – added to lancets, syringes and scalpels.

SEEING THE DOCTOR

Most patients were attended to at home, or they might come to the doctor's surgery. Hospitals were only used in the case of dire need. They were largely dirty and full of people with infectious diseases, which could not be cured. In the main, doctors did not make huge amounts of money. An average country GP might earn around £300 a year (more than Jane Austen's

father earned as a minister but substantially less than an aristocrat would need to live on). However, some very eminent doctors (and those who invented or discovered new cures or equipment) might earn considerably more than this.

Examination was the key to everything – although in some cases doctors did not presume on their patients in this way. When Queen Victoria became pregnant in the 1840s it was thought inappropriate for her to undergo medical examination. The diary of one lady at court tells of a group of royal physicians crowding the windows to watch the queen get into her carriage and, from that glimpse, trying to ascertain how far she was into her pregnancy.

With accurate diagnoses hard to reach, doctors often prescribed rest or a 'change of air', alongside purging of the body. This usually took the form of enemas (which had a laxative effect) or 'bleeding' the patient to release the 'impure humours'. Patients were 'bled' by applying either heated cups or live leeches to the skin, which, in fact, often weakened already sick people, hindering recovery. Poisons might also be applied, most notably mercury, which was injected or given orally. Effective advances were often achieved by chance and by observation more than by study or understanding their scientific basis. Jenner famously made his leap towards inoculation when he overheard milkmaids talking among themselves about how, having had the cowpox, they didn't suffer from its more serious sister disease, smallpox. Although the benefits of medical practitioners washing their hands had not yet been proven, in this era many doctors were noticing the difference this made and, in areas where they followed this practice, survival rates improved markedly.

However, many patients still died from diseases that today are completely preventable. A small cut or graze might become septic (and without antibiotics medical men were helpless). Likewise, flu or a bug might carry off a patient in a way that is unthinkable today. When a fuss is made in Jane Austen's stories about heroines getting wet in the rain or catching cold, it's worth bearing in mind that that kind of thing could be deadly. Tuberculosis was a constant danger. And hypochondriacs like Arthur and Diane in *Sanditon*, it could be argued, were simply keeping an eye out for the first signs of illnesses that could kill astonishingly quickly. Although the age of the plague was over, infectious diseases like typhoid and cholera regularly swept through the population (especially in towns), killing thousands at a time.

CHANCES OF SURVIVAL

Average life expectancy in the early 1800s in Britain was around forty years old. This does not mean that most people died at forty – if you survived childhood, you stood a good chance of making it to a relatively old age. If you were an adult woman, your greatest danger came in pregnancy and childbirth or from domestic violence, whereas when an adult man died in this era he was most likely to do so in battle or because of a workplace injury. Though forty seems very young to us today, this was an improvement on earlier rates of survival, as medical care improved little by little and nutrition became better for ordinary people. The quick uptake of the newly arrived potato to Britain during the 1600s is credited with helping to feed the working classes,

and advances in agriculture also made a contribution to raising the average age of death, as fewer people succumbed to illnesses associated with malnutrition.

The power of prayer was also an important part of the care given to sick people. Most people in Britain were practising Christians. In the absence of scientifically verified cures, trust was commonly put in God's mercy. Most hospitals were associated with a church, and ministers saw it as part of their job to visit the sick and comfort the families of those who were gravely ill. While Benjamin Franklin's famous remark 'God heals and the doctor takes the fee' is unfair, Georgian doctors probably harmed as much as they helped their patients and, on that basis, Lady Denham is quite right to resist the appointment of Dr Fuchs by Tom Parker as not being helpful to the health of those residing in Sanditon.

· • • ·

Wacky Georgian cures

LADY DENHAM: Good, good. And you drink the seawater as well?

CHARLOTTE: Er – not on purpose!

LADY DENHAM: Ah, you should, you should! I take half a tumbler of it every morning. *Episode 1*

DR FUCHS: My own little preparation – a light fard!

SIR EDWARD (s.v. to Esther): What do you suppose the purpose of a fard is?

ESTHER (s.v. to Edward): I think it is meant to extract impurities from the skin. And money from the gullible. *Episode 3*

The history of medicine is littered with strange potions, lotions and outlandish cures. The ancient Egyptians believed putting a dead mouse in your mouth would cure toothache

'*When I read about Regency recommendations for good health, I realised that wasn't much of a concern for Arthur Parker!*'

Turlough Convery, playing Arthur Parker

Tobacco

and in Mesopotamia in the millennia before Christ doctors diagnosed illness in their human patients by examining the entrails of sheep.

In Georgian England several 'cures' were anything but and Dr Fuchs' crazy treatments were all in use during the period. In fact, Fuchs' remedies offer only a taste of the worst that could happen if you put yourself into the care of a respectable Regency doctor.

To cure stuttering, some medical men recommended a hemiglossectomy, which meant that they cut off half the stutterer's tongue. This was done without anaesthetic and many patients bled to death.

Enemas were hugely popular for all kinds of complaints and were known as 'clysters' or 'glysters'. While enemas can be helpful in combating constipation, Georgians believed the treatment would cure all kinds of ailments, from strychnine poisoning to worms. It was thought of as one way to 'purge' the body of illness. Enemas were concocted from all sorts of odd ingredients (few of which would have any medical impact), including bran, honey, salt and tobacco.

Tobacco was hugely popular as a universal remedy. Called 'the holy herb', as well as being an ingredient in enemas and lotions it was smoked and snorted as 'snuff'. This was prescribed for a variety of illnesses, including headache, colds, asthma, nausea and exhaustion. The leaves of the plant were applied to treat burns, cuts, deafness, eye infections, constipation, boils, sores, croup, fluid retention, hair loss and animal bites. Tobacco smoke was also used to revive drowning victims – the last thing they would have needed – and was blown into the ear to relieve earache – again, no!

Tobacco was by no means the strangest medical ingredient used in the Georgian era. Arsenic was used in commonly available preparations to combat both malaria and syphilis – Fowler's solution was one arsenic formulation that claimed to cure both these diseases. Another, Donovan's solution, claimed to help arthritis and diabetes.

While some doctors made their own pills and potions by hand to their own recipes, there was also a system of patent medicines, which were advertised in newspapers and benefited from standardised production and pricing. Fowler's and Donovan's solutions were not efficacious, but some were based on relatively effective herbal cures. Willow provided an early form of aspirin. Coca leaves (in use in Britain during Shakespearian times as pipe tobacco) may also have been used as an ingredient, particularly for its power to numb pain – though cocaine wasn't isolated until well into the Victorian era.

Still, taking medical advice was a lottery. Beyond what would be seen today as basic first aid, doctors simply didn't have enough knowledge to be confident in prescribing for their patients. The worst of it was that, in tandem with direction to take the sea air or indulge in sea bathing, medical men would often apply several ineffective 'cures' at once – at best they didn't have any impact on a patient's health; at worst, they might make a condition more difficult to recover from. A sick person could easily find that they were subject to enemas (or other laxatives), being bled (see page 275) and a variety of patent medicines as their doctor struggled to provide any kind of useful remedy. And, to top it all off, they stood a good chance of being given a large measure of brandy to drink in one – also believed to be a general curative.

Willow

Cocoa

ARTHUR PARKER
Turlough Convery

ARTHUR PARKER:

If I were to be shipwrecked on a desert island with nothing but hot buttered toast and port wine, I should be quite contented.

– Episode 1

'The Parkers were no doubt a family of imagination and quick feelings . . . It would seem that they must either be very busy for the good of others or else extremely ill themselves.'

NARRATOR, *SANDITON*

Arthur Parker,
played by Turlough Convery

The youngest of the Parker brothers, Arthur and his sister Diana arrive in Sanditon to support Tom's project and attend the first Sanditon ball. He is a hypochondriac, constantly complaining of his ill health, but never showing any symptoms. A huge fan of food and drink (who loves buttered toast to the point of obsession), Arthur is bluff and easy-going, and, when push comes to shove, he has in all matters other than his own health a good head on his shoulders. He is a considerate and worthwhile friend to those around him.

Do you think Arthur means what he says about not being interested in marriage? What do you think it would take to win his heart?
Like most, Arthur could be won by the right person. Arthur enjoys the finer things in life and, if he could find a companion who he could eat hot buttered toast, drink port wine and laugh at the day's events with, he would be quite content, you know.

What is Arthur's ideal day?
Waking up past noon, a short (very short) stroll into town in search of fun, frolics and food, and ending the day with a spin around the dance floor. In fact, that sounds close to my ideal day too.

What is your favourite Jane Austen novel?
Pride and Prejudice and Zombies. *That was the original one, right?*

Which item of clothing from your costume might you wear in real life?

Without a doubt, it has to be my cape – it's iconic.

Arthur is obsessed with food . . . Are you getting sick of having to look like you're eating toast? And what is really in the port glasses?

Who would say no to eating as much as you like and being paid for it . . . As for what's in the port glasses, I presume it's Ribena (*hiccups*).

You've spoken out about women's rights in Northern Ireland. How do you feel about women's rights in the Regency?

One of the things we can acknowledge from the Regency to now is, yes, we've seen huge change since women were seen purely as property; however, this doesn't mean that we've finished the fight for full equal rights. Being from Northern Ireland, I've seen how the abortion laws affect women and our society as a whole. What brings me hope for change is the powerful campaigning by Alliance for Choice and London-Irish ARC and many more, which I would encourage everyone to get behind.

· • • ·

Attitudes to death

LADY DENHAM: You're a sharp one, Miss Heywood! But my relations all think they have a claim on it! The Breretons – I was a Miss Brereton – Miss Clara there is but one of many Breretons – and then there's Sir Harry's nephew and niece, Sir Edward Denham and Miss Esther! All of them hoping to do well by my demise! But there is one thing they all forget! And that is, that I have no intention at all of dying!   *Episode 1*

Death was very much part of day-to-day life for people in the Georgian era. While hospitals existed, most people recuperated from illness (and died) at home, where their bodies were laid out by family members, their servants or people hired specially to do so. Midwives sometimes supplemented their income by preparing bodies for burial. Mortality rates were high, particularly in childhood, and few people would not have seen the dead body of a loved one at close quarters. Removal of a corpse to a funeral parlour was a Victorian innovation, though in the Regency period the wealthy did

hire undertakers to organise funerary church services and burials. Until the funeral it was customary for someone to stay with the body – and members of the family would take turns to sit with their dead relation and keep a vigil.

Religion was an intrinsic part of life and most bodies were buried in their local graveyard. Burial in unconsecrated ground would have been considered scandalous, as would any practice other than burial (such as cremation). Criminals, including those who committed suicide, were not allowed the sanctuary of a burial in a churchyard and, as a result, it was commonly believed their souls could not reach heaven. This remained the case in the UK until suicide was decriminalised in 1961, though fully lifting the ban on church burials of suicides took even longer and was not completely revoked until 2017.

As you might imagine, avowed atheists in this era were uncommon. The philosopher David Hume, who died in 1776, was the talk of society, many people waiting for him to recant his lack of faith when he became ill. As Hume's health worsened and it was clear that he would die, the writer James Boswell paid him a visit to encourage him to admit there must be some kind of afterlife, but Hume remained consistent and died firm in the belief that there was no God and no heaven. This was extremely unusual.

Mortal illness was seen as something that had to be borne. Death announcements of the period often included the phrases 'resigned' or 'perfectly resigned' when referring to the final weeks or months of an invalid's life. It seems it was important to be seen to accept your fate and trust that the joys of heaven lay ahead. The concept of 'a good death' appears regularly in correspondence and other writing of the period.

Outside of the main towns the dead were transported to the local church along medieval byways known as 'corpse roads'. Bodies were always carried along these country roads with their feet pointing away from home, and it was traditional that the route had to cross water so that bad spirits could not follow. Again, most corpses would be accompanied by their closest relations, although in upper-class Georgian society often the women of the household did not perform this function. The dead could not be admitted to the churchyard without a priest being present and in country churches you often see a porch at the gate to the graveyard, which was where people sheltered with their loved ones until the priest came to accompany them onto consecrated ground.

Tokens of remembrance were often handed out at the funeral or in the days following it. Rosemary sprigs or black handkerchiefs were common examples of this practice, but wealthy mourners might buy mourning jewellery (often made of jet) or commission 'hair jewellery' (jewellery that included a lock of the dead person's hair in its construction) – as Cassandra Austen did when Jane died in 1817, to commemorate her memory.

ESTHER DENHAM
Charlotte Spencer

ESTHER:
All in all I think you might regret ever setting a foot in Sanditon. I know
I do.

– Episode 1

---

*'And Miss Esther must marry somebody of fortune too.
She must get a rich husband. Ah, young ladies that
have no money very much to be pitied!'*
LADY DENHAM, *SANDITON*

Esther Denham, played by Charlotte Spencer

Esther lives with her brother, Edward. Both Denhams are in Sanditon to try to secure their inheritance from Lady Denham. Manipulative in the extreme, Esther is highly skilled in placing casual comments which sting like a barb. Apart from being in thrall to Edward, she has Clara Brereton's claim to what she sees as her inheritance within her sights. A formidable foe, she has no interest in anything outside her own concerns, so when prospective suitors present themselves she rejects them out of hand.

One of Esther's problems as a character is that she is too honest, isn't it?

Esther is so honest and I think it's beautiful. People are very concerned with how they are perceived all the time so to see a character who is candid is like breathing in the freshest of air!

The relationship between Esther and Edward is extraordinarily (and a little weirdly) close, isn't it?

Edward is Esther's best friend. He is the only man she has closely known, who has conversations with her and seems to value her opinion. That's not to say she couldn't find that with another man.

What was the favourite scene you shot during the series?

The ball scene. I had so much fun; it was like a dream! The whole thing was lit by candlelight, there was a live band and I personally absolutely love to dance, so I was in my element!

What did you learn that you didn't know before about life in the Regency?

I learned nothing I didn't already know. That beneath all the pretence of the men, the women were running the show.

What was your favourite line and why?

There are so many of Esther's lines that I love (especially when she's cutting), for example: 'Did you hear that, Edward? Parasitic worms. We could call this one Clara'.

· • • • ·

Fainting

The only time we know Jane Austen fainted (from her letters) was when her father announced that he was retiring and the family was to move from Steventon to Bath in 1801. However, many of her female characters faint – often to comic purpose. Mrs Bennet in *Pride and Prejudice* responds to any crisis with a 'fit of the vapors', nerves or a fainting spell, and Louisa Musgrove in *Persuasion* develops a habit of fainting into her boyfriend's arms, on one occasion knocking herself unconscious on the paving stones when she falls. Once her sister faints at the same time, causing a crowd to form: 'the workmen and boatmen about the Cobb, and many were collected . . . to enjoy the sight of a dead young lady, nay, two dead young ladies, for it proved twice as fine as the first report'.

In all these cases, fainting (or almost fainting) is a response to a stressful situation and, indeed, Georgian women had relatively few ways of taking control of what was going on around them – fainting and fits being one of them. Although it is likely some fainting fits were not genuine, it is entirely possible that many were. Fainting is commonly associated with a lack of oxygen. Women usually wore 'stays' or corsets during the Regency era, which could trigger fainting episodes brought on by lack of breath. Fainting has also been associated with arsenic poisoning

Nineteenth-century enamelled gold smelling salts boxes.

and the early stages of some illnesses, as well as dehydration and low blood pressure.

If you fainted you would be revived with 'smelling salts', or more likely with a 'vinaigrette', which was a small box (often made from silver) that contained a vinegar-soaked sponge. Many women carried these with them at all times in their reticules. Vinegar was a 'go-to' medicine in the Georgian era – used in households for cleaning and as a general antibacterial agent. Sometimes these sponges were fitted into the head of a walking cane. Other aromatic substances might be used along with the vinegar – cinnamon, rosemary or lavender. If you fainted, the strong smell of the vinegar made you take a sharp breath, which would revive you. 'Hungary water' might also be applied – this was simply scented water that could be dabbed onto the skin – a little like the summertime cooling sprays we use today. Vinaigrettes were also useful against offensive smells in town, where the streets were extremely dirty, littered with horse and dog (and sometimes human) excrement and other slurry. In some areas rubbish might also be thrown out of the window (including the contents of bed pans).

In polite society, fainting women were laid out to recover on a day bed, also known as a chaise longue or a fainting couch. Most grand houses had one of these in the drawing room, which, when not occupied by an unconscious lady, could simply be used like a sofa. You can see one on the *Sanditon* set in Lady Denham's drawing room.

'Beware of fainting-fits . . . One fatal swoon has cost me my life . . . Beware of swoons, dear Laura . . . a frenzy fit is not one quarter so pernicious; it is an exercise to the body and if not too violent, is, I dare say, conducive to health in its consequences – Run mad as often as you choose; but do not faint.'

Love and Freindship,
Jane Austen

The story of
Dr James Miranda Barry:
a nineteenth-century scandal

With Jane Austen's enquiring mind, she probably would have relished the opportunity of going to university had it been available to her, but formal higher education was closed to women during the Regency. This did not mean that all women simply accepted this constraint. When a woman named Margaret Ann Bulkley – born in Cork, Ireland, in 1789 – decided she wanted to study medicine in 1809, aided by her family she simply dressed as a man and took the name James Miranda Barry before travelling to Scotland and forging this new identity. Some at the medical faculty at Edinburgh University were suspicious that this Irishman was too young for the course on account of his unbroken voice, slight build and the fact he did not need to shave, but they did not suspect the truth. In 1812, when it was time for Barry to graduate, the university senate had to be persuaded to allow him to pass by a friend of Barry's family, the Earl of Buchan, who argued that Barry simply seemed young – but that he was no younger than many students (at this stage Barry was in his early twenties). The earl's argument was successful and Barry became an MD, going on to study in

London and passing the final exams at the Royal College of Surgeons of England the following year.

James Miranda Barry kept his secret for the rest of his life, and went on to have a distinguished career as an army doctor, receiving promotion after promotion. He practised in Chelsea and at the Royal Military Hospital in Plymouth before going on to Cape Town, South Africa, where he became the personal physician of the governor. In 1822 he became Colonial Medical Inspector there and was responsible for improving sanitation and water supply, as well as setting up a leper colony. Barry was also an early adherent of the Caesarean section and performed one of the first successful operations where both mother and child survived.

Dr James Miranda Barry.

Barry was clearly an extremely competent physician and a good administrator of public health measures. More promotions were forthcoming, as were postings in the West Indies, Mauritius, Corfu and the Crimea, where, although Barry improved conditions, he fell out with Florence Nightingale over practices at her Scutari hospital. His philosophy and medical skills were at the cutting edge for the times: Barry constantly stood up for better conditions and food for ordinary soldiers and facilities for the poor and sick, including (unusually) for the mentally ill. Barry lived an entirely teetotal life and was a vegetarian. He was extremely fond of his poodle, Psyche, and had a black manservant, John Joseph Danson, who was engaged during Barry's early posting in South Africa and stayed with him for the rest of his life.

When Barry died in 1865, he left instructions that his body should not be subjected to a postmortem or 'any examination', and that he should be buried in the bedsheets he died on. The doctor in attendance (who had known Barry for several years) issued a death certificate that identified him as male, but later, a cleaning lady who was laying out the body, saw Barry naked and brought the matter to public attention. It was considered so shocking that the British Army sealed Barry's records for 100 years.

Argument rages to this day over whether Barry was a transgender man or simply a woman who disguised herself in order to undertake what was an extraordinary and hugely successful medical and military career. Either way, as a woman, Barry would not have been able to live the life he chose and gain the education he did – the first person who was born female to qualify and practise as a doctor in modern times – several decades before any other woman managed to do so.

· • • ·

What's for dinner?

Diet in Georgian Britain depended on class. In working- and lower-class households where there were no servants, cooking was done usually over a fire in one pot. Porridge, soups and stews were the most common meals. Meat was expensive and was used sparingly and as a luxury – a spit-roast piece of meat (a joint or whole chicken) might have been a treat but one that was affordable for most people now and then. Alcohol consumption was relatively high as the water was not clean, and weak beer was the drink of choice for working-class people with all their meals. This sometimes led to drunkenness, which was not an exclusively working-class issue: judges, in particular, were known to overindulge, drinking wine during the day and then passing sentence on prisoners.

In upper-class houses there was a separate kitchen that was run by a cook who was in charge of any number of kitchen maids, kitchen boys and sous-chefs. A continental head chef was a status symbol and during the Regency there were advances in technology, which meant cooking ranges were introduced in large houses. At the same time, porcelain became more common and large dinner services were the vogue. The poor ate from wooden, tin or pewter plates.

Many upper-class families owned estates that housed

farms, allowing them to produce their own food, including homegrown fruit and vegetables and milk, butter and cheeses from the family dairy. Buying in a pineapple as a curiosity was very expensive, as Lady Denham makes clear during her pineapple luncheon – commonly, a single pineapple would cost a guinea to rent and two guineas if you wanted to also eat it. With transport times too long to import exotic fruit from anywhere it would grow in the wild, pineapples had to be grown in a greenhouse, the preserve of the highest aristocracy and of institutions like Kew Gardens. There was a roaring trade in seeds and cuttings to grow both staple vegetables and more exotic treats.

Day to day, most characters in *Sanditon* would take

a late breakfast, enjoying tea, coffee or even hot chocolate, all of which were luxuries the poor could not afford. Pastries were popular at breakfast time, as was smoked fish, like kippers, and eggs. White bread was preferred to brown, as white flour was more expensive and believed to be easier on the digestion. Because breakfast was eaten late, lunch was not a large meal and was often viewed as more for women than men (who by lunchtime were generally out and about on their business). Dinner for the upper classes was the main event of the day. This was a lavish spread and usually lasted for several hours. Many different dishes were eaten together; it was not unusual for beef, chicken, pork and lamb all to appear on the menu in the evening. Game was a status symbol: to have grouse, partridge or venison, you had to have access to a shooting estate. On menus of the period this spread would be considered a single course, which in the Georgian era was not a single dish but a choice of many platters spread across the table from which the diners could choose, like a seated buffet. If you were by the sea or a river, fish would also be included on the menu. Oysters were so common they were considered a working-class food, as was lobster.

Puddings were hugely popular. Sugar was imported from the West Indies – Jane Austen herself wrote to her sister, Cassandra, about her sweet tooth: 'You know how interesting the purchase of a sponge-cake is to me.' Combine this luxury with ice (you had to be very wealthy to have access to ice, which you might collect over the winter and store in a specially built 'ice house') and the vogue for ice cream was born. The upper classes did not drink beer, instead importing wine, port and Madeira (sweet wine), which could only be bought by the case, keeping these luxuries out of the financial reach of most people. During the Napoleonic Wars buying French goods was considered unpatriotic and fortified wines became extremely popular, as they were imported from Portugal, a long-standing ally and trading partner. Many officers brought their taste for Portuguese and Spanish wine and food home from the war, having fought through these countries and up through the south of France during the Duke of Wellington's Peninsular campaign.

After dinner, tea was served. Afternoon tea was not yet a normal occurrence. Tea was also drunk with supper at public events in the assembly rooms, where you'd almost certainly be able to buy negus – a hot punch made from port, water, sugar, lemon and nutmeg, which was popular at balls and dance parties. White soup was also frequently served at balls, and features in *Pride and Prejudice*. This was a chicken and bacon soup thickened with almonds, bread and cream.

While being well fed was to be aspired to, it's no wonder, with all this rich fare on offer, overeating was rife. Being overweight was seen as a health problem. The Prince Regent himself was hugely fat and satirical magazines mocked his lavish lifestyle. The regent's political enemies ridiculed his size and particularly criticised his affection for 'foreign foods', which were portrayed as inferior to British roasts and puddings. Since the mid-1700s there had been some medical backing for weight-loss diets to help combat illness. There were several famous diet doctors who touted pills and potions said to help the weak-willed lose the pounds, and newspaper advertisements brought these within the reach of ordinary people, who might not be able to afford a doctor.

WHAT IS A SEASON?

· · · ·

Originally, the 'season' was linked to the months that the House of Commons and House of Lords sat in Westminster. This was the time that the upper classes converged upon London – from October or November until the beginning of the summer, May or June, when the weather improved. Entertainments were staged for the families of men engaged in political activity, who joined them in the capital, bringing eligible single children in the hope they would make a match. In the summer, the upper classes would then leave London to go to their estates where they would stay to oversee the harvest.

As the condition of Britain's roads improved, the season shifted forward a couple of months because it was possible to travel more easily to and from London over the winter. By the Regency era, the season might start in January or February and go on later, until July or even August. It was also expected that the royal family would be in London for some of the months that Parliament sat – often October to December and then from April to July. These were 'hot spots' in the season when a hostess might hope to tempt royal guests to her events, giving her and her family additional social cachet.

In a seaside town, like Sanditon, however, when residents refer to the 'season' they are talking about the summertime. Sea bathing, one of the main attractions of a resort, was only tolerable over the summer when the weather was warmer. A Sanditon season, therefore, might run from April to August when, with the town's close proximity to London, fashionable society could be tempted down to take the waters.

1819 IN SANDITON AND THE WORLD BEYOND

APRIL

- Charlotte Heyworth arrives in Sanditon.

- Lady Denham's Pineapple Luncheon.

- The Sanditon opening ball.

- The French slave ship, Bonny, sets off from Africa. All slaves on the ship were thrown overboard after everyone on the ship became blind through illness.

MAY

- Memphis, Tennessee, is founded.

- Queen Victoria is born but is not considered close enough to the succession to come to the throne.

- The first bicycles (known as swiftwalkers) arrive in New York.

JUNE

· An earthquake in Gujarat, India,
kills over 1500 people.

· The notorious Strathnever clearances
begin on the Duke of Sutherland's
Highland estate.

JULY

- *Astronomer Johann Tralles discovers what becomes known as the Great Comet of 1819.*

- *The cabinet consider and reject pursuing the regent's wife, Caroline of Brunswick, for adultery as they consider it would be an embarrassment to the nation.*

AUGUST

- The Peterloo Massacre takes place in Manchester, where peaceful demonstrators are charged by troops.

- Colombia becomes independent of Spanish rule.

- James Watt, inventor of the steam engine, dies.

- Prince Albert, who will marry Queen Victoria, is born in Germany.

- The first parachute jump in America takes place.

- Allan Pinkerton, founder of the Pinkerton Detective Agency, is born in Scotland.

Did we do Jane Austen proud?

We hope you enjoyed *Sanditon*.

The whole team loved dipping into the Regency period and lifting the curtain on all of the glamour and some of the grit that made up the complicated world Jane Austen lived in.

Whether your favourite was the romance, the dialogue, the seaside or the costumes, the actors and the production crew always appreciate the interest of series fans.

For *Sanditon* news, find updates online at:

Instagram – @Sanditon_official,
Facebook – @SanditonOfficial,
Twitter – @Sanditon

Not ready to leave the world of Sanditon yet? . . .

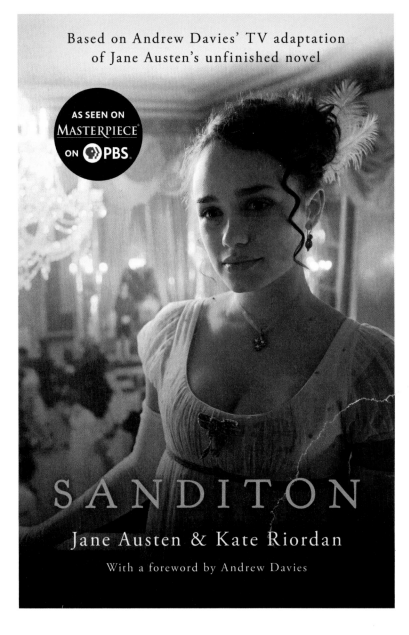

Based on Andrew Davies' TV adaptation
of Jane Austen's unfinished novel

AS SEEN ON
MASTERPIECE
ON PBS

SANDITON

Jane Austen & Kate Riordan

With a foreword by Andrew Davies

PICTURE CREDITS

Grand Central Publishing
Hachette Book Group
1290 Avenue of the Americas, New York, NY 10104
grandcentralpublishing.com
twitter.com/grandcentralpub

First published in Great Britain in 2019 by Trapeze, an imprint of The Orion Publishing Group Ltd. Carmelite House, 50 Victoria Embankment, London EC4Y 0DZ. An Hachette UK company.

First US Edition: December 2019

Grand Central Publishing is a division of Hachette Book Group, Inc. The Grand Central Publishing name and logo is a trademark of Hachette Book Group, Inc.

Book interior designed by Clare Sivell and Helen Ewing

Library of Congress Control Number: 2019949695

ISBNs: 978-1-5387-3471-1 (hardcover); 978-1-5387-3470-4 (ebook)

Printed in the United States of America

LSC-C

10 9 8 7 6 5 4 3 2 1